THINK BIGGER

The Bloomberg Financial Series provides both core reference knowledge and actionable information for financial professionals. The books are written by experts familiar with the workflows, challenges, and demands of investment professionals who trade the markets, manage money, and analyze investments in their capacity of growing and protecting wealth, hedging risk, and generating revenue.

Since 1996, Bloomberg Press has published books for financial professionals on investing, economics, and policy affecting investors. Titles are written by leading practitioners and authorities, and have been translated into more than 20 languages.

For a list of available titles, please visit our website at www.wiley.com/go/bloombergpress.

THINK BIGGER

And 39 Other Winning Strategies from Successful Entrepreneurs

**Michael W. Sonnenfeldt,
Founder, Tiger 21**

WILEY

Published by John Wiley & Sons, Inc., Hoboken, New Jersey.
Published simultaneously in Canada.

For general information on our other products and services or for technical support, please contact our Customer Care Department within the United States at (800) 762-2974, outside the United States at (317) 572-3993, or fax (317) 572-4002.

Wiley publishes in a variety of print and electronic formats and by print-on-demand. Some material included with standard print versions of this book may not be included in e-books or in print-on-demand. If this book refers to media such as a CD or DVD that is not included in the version you purchased, you may download this material at http://booksupport.wiley.com. For more information about Wiley products, visit www.wiley.com.

Library of Congress Cataloging-in-Publication Data

Names: Sonnenfeldt, Michael W., author.
Title: Think bigger : and 39 other winning strategies from successful
    entrepreneurs / Michael W. Sonnenfeldt.
Description: Hoboken, New Jersey : John Wiley & Sons, Inc., [2017] | Includes
    index. |
Identifiers: LCCN 2017023335 (print) | LCCN 2017036162 (ebook) | ISBN
    978-1-119-42633-2 (pdf) | ISBN 978-1-119-42632-5 (epub) | ISBN 978-1-119-42631-8
    (cloth)
Subjects: LCSH: New business enterprises. | Entrepreneurship. | Success in
    business.
Classification: LCC HD62.5 (ebook) | LCC HD62.5 .S6753 2017 (print) | DDC
    658.4/09–dc23
LC record available at https://lccn.loc.gov/2017023335

Printed in the United States of America.

SKY10031500_111821

Contents

STAGE 2: TEAM BUILDING

STAGE 3: RISK MANAGEMENT

STAGE 4: GROWING YOUR BUSINESS THE SMART WAY

STAGE 5: PROTECTING YOUR WEALTH

Acknowledgments

Writing a book like this was a challenge beyond what I could have imagined. I have learned things about the unique nature of some very successful entrepreneurs through the intimate experiences I shared with fellow members of Tiger 21 over the past two decades. Translating and clarifying those insights into a book that would be of interest to others was where the real challenge lay.

I knew I would need to partner with a writer who not only could focus more intently on this project than my schedule would allow but also bring skills I did not have. My agent, Jim Levine, introduced me to Ed Tivnan, a deeply experienced reporter and writer. Ed had the skills and experience writing books and interviewing people—something I simply lacked. Our original focus was to capture the insights I had been developing and see what was there. As we built an initial collection of ideas and themes, it was clear that we needed to conduct more interviews with Tiger 21 members to see how their experiences could lead us to further insights. We spent a full year pursuing and digesting interviews. Ed handled the majority of them and eventually realized the best way to organize all of these insights was through the vehicle of a *lesson book*. What seems obvious now was not at all obvious then.

While my own story is woven throughout the book, and I knew of or identified many of the interviewees through the help of the Tiger 21 chairs who lead and facilitate each of our 35 groups, Ed did the heavy lifting for much of the book. Yes, it is my story, but his efforts are all over it. I could not have made the progress I did without his terrific work on the project.

When I thought we were done, I had the good fortune, through my close friend and book mentor Seth Siegel (who helped with just about every major decision I made on this book), to be introduced to Bari Weiss, a young superstar book review editor then at the *Wall Street Journal*. I was curious how she thought the book would be received, but after reading it, she immediately commented that we had not included enough stories about women entrepreneurs and any unique lessons they might have to share. Bingo! In my initial rush to capture as many stories as possible, I didn't think about the mix of the interviewees. Fortunately, Bari and I were able to capture a few important stories from Tiger 21 members who were women. I am enormously grateful for Bari's additional insights and the interviews she did that added the voices of more of our female members.

In addition to the many editing changes Bari made, I also received important editing suggestions from Arthur Goldwag at a critical time in the book's development, and from Christina Verigan, assigned to me by Wiley. Then the production team at Wiley really put the finishing touches on the book with their deft editing.

Throughout the project, Kathleen Dunleavy, with whom I have had the pleasure of working for 30 years, kept me on track with all the details I would have otherwise have missed. As usual, her assistance was simply invaluable, and I could not have gotten through the myriad of details without her. She has been the most constant professional colleague of my career, without whose help I would be lost most of the time.

However, my deepest appreciation goes to the many members of Tiger 21 who were kind enough to share their stories with me and share the insights that their extraordinary careers allowed them to develop. Not all of them made it into the book, but even those that didn't have helped me learn important lessons I might not have ever been exposed to. Learning from fellow members has been one of the primary joys of my life for the past 20 years. I am endlessly fascinated by my fellow members' stories and ever grateful for their willingness to share in a way that I, and other members, can learn from and grow. Not only were the many chairs at Tiger 21 helpful in identifying members with great stories, but a few of them also shared their own important experiences. (Thank you, Cal Simmons, Barbara Roberts, Charlie Garcia, and Chris Ryan, for your stories and insights.) I also want to recognize the key professionals on the Tiger 21 staff with whom I have worked for the last decade and more. We could not have created the platform from which this book springs without your creativity, dedication, and brilliant execution.

A first book project is an entirely new experience, and at each stage, expectations have to recalibrated. My agent, Jim Levine, has been a great guide along the way. We were extremely lucky to have received interest from Steve Isaacs at Bloomberg Books, and Tula Weis and Sheck Cho at Wiley. I am indebted to the whole Bloomberg and Wiley teams for giving me this opportunity.

I am sure I have forgotten or omitted many others along the way whose insights added immeasurably to the finished product. Over the past three years, I sought and received input from countless people, many of whom made critical differences along the way. Thanks to all of you.

While I am primarily responsible for the creation and evolution of Tiger 21, as an organization, it has grown far beyond my specific contributions. My initial partner, Richard Lavin, ran Tiger 21 for its first five years. His attention to detail and commitment to the concept allowed us to get up and running. He taught me a lesson based on his deep restaurant experience: Kiss your customers on all four cheeks. We simply could not have grown into the organization we have become today without Richard's initial participation. Then Tommy Gallagher stepped in. In a remarkably short time, Tommy took a small New York–based organization and created a national footprint. We saw remarkable increases in our membership and our staff during his tenure. Tommy has been a steadfast partner for almost all of Tiger 21's history, and one of my best friends to boot. I have been pleased to share this journey with him. In 2009, Jonathan Kempner joined Tiger 21 as president and brought experience we simply never had. While providing a steady hand for the six years he was at the helm, he was almost always a real pleasure to work with. When he insisted on developing our annual conference, despite my objections, it turned out to be one of the most transformational activities in our 20-year history. Jonathan forever changed Tiger 21 with his insights about how to build a large organization and how best to serve our members interests'. We now are being led by Barbara Goodstein as CEO, and under her leadership, we are growing even faster. We have just opened London, and I can't wait to see what evolves in the coming years.

I have had the good fortune of being associated with Harley Frank for almost 35 years. Over that time period, we have worked together in almost every business I have been involved with, and he has always brought a unique perspective and unmatched creative energy. The idea of translating the wisdom from our members' experiences into a book was Harley's, and for a number of years he relentlessly pushed me to write it. Without Harley's initial energy pushing me forward in the early stages, there would never have been a book. Harley impresses me with his interesting, creative one-off marketing, branding, and promotional ideas more than anyone else in my orbit. While I hope this book turns out to be the best of them, it is only one of many of his ideas that I have benefited from over all these years.

Finally, it is my wife, Katja, and our four children to whom I am personally most indebted. All the sacrifices, schedule changes, trip cancellations, missed dinners, interrupted dinners, and endless distractions that my personality has driven me to accept have most often come at the expense of spending time with each of them, and most of all, with Katja. Without their support, encouragement, acquiescence, and acceptance, the activities and events I have shared in this book, and the book itself, would never have come to be. For that and so much more I am forever grateful.

Introduction

Every year in the United States, half a million men and women decide to take the biggest risk of their lives in pursuit of a dream. To get there, some of them take out a second mortgage on their homes. Some of them wipe out their savings. Others borrow money or seek investments from friends and family. Some drop out of college. Others uproot their families. And some leave high-paying jobs with corner offices at prestigious companies.

They all do this in order to start a business of their own. To be their own boss. To create jobs for people in their communities. To make something entirely new, or perhaps just something much more efficient. And, yes, frequently with the hope of making millions of dollars.

These risk-takers decide to leap despite the fact that the odds they face are, by any reasonable measure, absolutely dismal. About two-thirds of the businesses they start, according to the Small Business Administration, will fail within 10 years. And that's a sunny estimate! *Forbes* magazine claims that the number of deaths is closer to 90 percent.[1] A Harvard Business School professor recently studied 10 years of data on more than 2,000 start-ups that were so well planned and positioned that they received venture capital funding. But even 75 percent of these best picks failed to return their initial capital.

When you read those statistics it seems a miracle that so many Americans even try to start a business, knowing it might mean going broke; losing money borrowed from family, friends, and investors; or potentially damaging or destroying their reputations.

Who are these seemingly delusional people who dwell among us? We have a fancy word for them—*entrepreneurs*—but that title doesn't begin to capture this unique breed of exceptionally gritty people.

Chances are when you hear the word *entrepreneur* you think of Facebook's Mark Zuckerberg in his Harvard dorm room or Apple's two Steves (Jobs and Wozniak) tinkering in a Los Altos garage. Or perhaps the scrappier startups of *Shark Tank* leap to mind.

Me? I think of people like Gary Mendell, who started flipping burgers and went on to build a hotel management and development company that sold a $300 million hotel portfolio to Starwood. Or of Pete Settle, a lawyer and engineer, who founded a school-bus company that became one of the nation's largest student-transportation providers. I think of Will Ade, who lost his job at a Texas oil firm and started his own wildcat exploration consultancy based in Singapore, giving him a net worth beyond anything he could have ever dreamed of.

If you've picked up this book, chances are you see yourself as a future Zuckerberg or Jobs or Mendell or Settle or Ade. Or perhaps you're wondering if you have what it takes to become a professional daredevil.

Maybe you're a bit further along your journey—5 or 10 years into your successful startup. You're wondering whether or not to sell or go public and finding that even though you've got lots of friends in finance, their advice is coming up short. Or maybe you're like me: a person who's built a successful career on taking risks that others deemed crazy.

I got in the game at 24 years old after two jobs. I wanted to pursue a real estate development opportunity that I had been noodling on since I was 17, right after I dropped out of freshman year at the University of Michigan. That summer, I was working in a warehouse on the Jersey City waterfront. Only a few thousand feet across the Hudson River from the end of the pier where I took my lunch breaks, Wall Street was bursting at the seams with new data centers and expanding operations. Those expansions were starting to leapfrog the Jersey waterfront to remote suburban campuses, which felt like Siberia to employees. The railroads had owned most of the Jersey waterfront across from Manhattan, and their midcentury bankruptcies and reorganizations had blinded developers to the obvious advantages of setting up data centers and back offices five minutes from Wall Street.

My idea was so bold that most real estate veterans did not think anyone could pull it off—never mind a no-name twenty-something who'd never developed anything in his life. I wanted to convert a rundown, 2.5-million-square-foot warehouse into the new home for lower Manhattan's high-tech office expansion plans.

After 18 months and a couple of false starts, the $25 million deal went through and the Harborside Terminal quickly became America's largest commercial renovation project. Little could I have known that the project, which over the next three decades evolved into a mixed-use office, retail, hotel, and condominium complex, would be viewed as a vanguard in terms of waterfront development and one of the most successful real estate deals in New York metropolitan history.

Four and half years after we bought Harborside, my partner and I cashed out. We had achieved a level of success beyond anything we could have imagined.

In the decades that followed, I had a few more victories, but I also endured some painful defeats. Along the way I was forced to come to grips with my own limitations. If you're smarting from a business that went bust or learning the hard lesson of what *risky* really means, trust me. I've been there.

One important lesson I realized early on was that the undergraduate and graduate degrees I proudly earned at MIT's Sloan School (after returning to college following an 18-month stint of work I did after dropping out of Michigan) rarely provided the critical difference in the making of a deal. Don't get me wrong, having B.S. and M.S. degrees from MIT has been one of the fastest ways to build credibility during my career, and the amazing education I received there gave me perspective and knowledge that I could not have easily duplicated elsewhere, and I am proud, to this day, to be an MIT alum. But what saved me, time and time again, wasn't my education, but the wisdom of other people who had already been through something I was wrestling with for the first time and their perspectives gained over decades of experiences I was yet to have.

See, that first deal of mine would never have happened without my mentor and partner, David Fromer. He was twice my age: I was in high school while the Vietnam War was raging; David had won three Purple Hearts and a Bronze Star during World War II. He'd then spent 30 years buying, building, and selling real estate in Los Angeles, London, and Saudi Arabia. Without David's wisdom, experience, and penchant for risk taking, that New Jersey waterfront project, and all the dozens of deals that came after that for me, wouldn't have been possible.

Common wisdom has it that the best teacher is experience. Indeed, in my 40-year career as an entrepreneur, I have found that the best teacher is experience—*someone else's experience.* Each and every time, what helped me build multiple businesses (and nonprofit organizations, too) was the hard-won advice of other entrepreneurs.

Nineteen years ago, after I sold my second company, I felt that I was more than a little at sea, and I was in desperate need of advice from others who had traveled the same road before me.

I decided to do something about it.

The Investment Group for Enhanced Results in the 21st Century (Tiger 21)—what is today the premier peer-to-peer learning network for high-net-worth wealth creators in North America—was the result. It began with a single group of six entrepreneurs in New York City who had all sold their businesses. All of us were post our *liquidity event*, and we all felt challenged to wisely preserve our wealth, while also exploring issues of relevance, legacy, family, philanthropy, and the big *what's next*.

It turns out that I wasn't the only entrepreneur who craved the advice and community that only fellow entrepreneurs could provide. Unlike those who work in hedge funds, banks, or traditional businesses, entrepreneurs lack the structure and institutional knowledge that these more established businesses provide.

Entrepreneurs need guidance—and not just when they're starting out. They need guidance when they're growing their companies and pulling them through the inevitable crises that pop up. Those lucky few whose businesses become valuable enough to sell need it even more. The right advice can position a sale to yield multiples of after-tax or philanthropic dollars that might have been lost because of poor planning or missed opportunities. It can save an entrepreneur from jumping into a sale prematurely and help prepare him or her for what comes next—which is often even more challenging. There are any number of people and firms who will offer you investment and management advice for a price. But objective, disinterested guidance from fellow entrepreneurs who have already built and sold companies of their own is awfully hard to come by.

Today, Tiger 21 has grown beyond my wildest expectations. We have 40 groups in 35 cities across the United States and Canada. All told, our 500-plus members have a collective net worth of over $50 billion (and control assets with value in excess of $100 billion, when you add the financial and real estate assets some of them manage for others). We are currently expanding around the globe. Our first London group convened in the spring of 2017.

Although we have our share of current and former partners in Wall Street firms and major real estate companies who bring critical insights from the front lines of finance to our meetings, the majority of our members—some of whom you will meet in these pages—made their fortunes on Main Street, in fields ranging from coin-operated washing machines and medical supplies to payday loans, tax liens, and legal services. The majority of them come from working- and middle-class families; many are still friends with their high school classmates. Most are justifiably uncomfortable about discussing the unique challenges and opportunities that come from having made it big, and when they do open up, they tend to be more inclined to talk about their screwups than their successes.

Once a month, all of us break away from our businesses, investments, philanthropies, hobbies, and families to spend the day speaking frankly and confidentially with one another about everything relating to our businesses and even our lives and families. Many members refer to Tiger 21 as their "personal board of directors"—their most reliable source for honest, no-holds-barred advice in just about every important aspect of their lives. I've come to think of it as a one-of-a-kind laboratory of success.

This book started when I asked myself a question: What have I learned from my nearly 20 years of intimate connection to some of North America's most successful and creative entrepreneurs?

A lot, it turns out. Beyond the business tips and investment advice and support that I was looking for in the beginning, I've gained a deep and highly personal understanding of what makes me and other entrepreneurs tick—knowledge that would be incredibly useful to anyone who has their own idea for a startup, is building a business, is thinking about selling one, or who already has.

Access to this formidable brain trust generally requires a minimum of $10 million in investible assets and an annual fee of $30,000. Until now! In the following pages I will take you deep inside our exclusive network—and happily waive the fee.

Sharing this wisdom has never been more important. That's because we are at a very precarious economic and political moment in our nation's history. The wealth gap between the rich and poor is starker than ever. And our country's once-thriving middle class is eroding, largely thanks to globalization and the advent of brilliant new technologies.

Concern over the lack of good jobs here at home reached a fever pitch during the 2016 presidential election, in which candidates of both parties promised to bring jobs back—even if it meant passing protectionist policies that, in reality, would actually harm the very people they are trying to help. Such promises create false hopes.

The hard truth is that the jobs that have been offshored to China, Mexico, and the rest of the developing world only represent about 15 percent of the job losses everyone is talking about. The rest—85 percent—were gobbled up by automation. No one is going to retire the robots that play a growing role in our factories. No one is going to unlearn the technology behind self-driving cars, and no one is going to unplug the computers that run so much of our lives.

If we want to create jobs in this country, we can't look to steep tariffs on imports or impenetrable borders. We need to look to entrepreneurs.

Historically, entrepreneurs have created many of the private-sector jobs that have underpinned our economy, contributing mightily to the steepest rise in standards of living that the world has ever seen. The same has been true of the past 70 years. Jobs haven't primarily been created by the big, established firms, but by the entrepreneurial enterprises that continue to be the engine of American economic growth.

This will be the case even more in the future. The primary source of new, sustainable jobs will be small companies founded by entrepreneurs, some of which will grow into behemoths in the years to come.

Those entrepreneurs will need all the support they can get from political leaders in Washington and statehouses across the nation. Some would define the challenge as removing all the obstacles that have been erected. The problem is that right now, far too many members of the political class, even the most pro-business among them, have a faulty understanding of who entrepreneurs are and why they do what they do. My hope is that the stories in this book will give policy makers a better understanding of how we tick and, thus, what we—as a country—need the most.

Entrepreneurs are not saints, of course, nor are we public servants, even though the enterprises we've created have contributed mightily to our nation's prosperity.

But if working on this book has taught me anything, it is that successful entrepreneurs *are* a special species in the world of business. They are different from corporate leaders (though many of the best entrepreneurs are also great leaders) and from professional investors (though many talented investors have built their own companies). And while the best entrepreneurs do display certain psychological and character traits that are common to success stories in other fields—like self-discipline, grit, and tolerance for risk—I would bet that if you took a random sample of entrepreneurs, you would find that the most successful among us tend to have even higher levels of those traits, supercharged by an optimism that psychologists would label *delusional.* When you add to that mix the ambition that a poor or lower-middle-class background or a broken home can nurture, a unique set of traits comes into focus.

If you come up short on too many of those traits, even years of study, planning, and dedication will not suffice to make you an entrepreneur. But if you do have them—and I suspect you might if you picked up this book—you can cultivate and develop them.

To those people who can't stomach the idea of going back to school, or formal education in general, take heart: Many of the most successful entrepreneurs I know are not book smart, but are quite brilliant in their own ways, and they are often particularly well endowed with a level of emotional intelligence that makes them inspiring leaders. They are often endlessly curious, too. I've also detected a high incidence of learning issues, such as dyslexia and attention deficit disorder, among entrepreneurs. It seems the more obstacles they have successfully overcome, the more likely entrepreneurial success becomes.

One of the most important lessons I've learned can be summed up in a quote from David Russell, one of our original Tiger 21 members: "When I was young, they used to say on TV, 'The smart money is doing this, the smart money is doing that.' I finally got to be wealthy, and I find out that 'the smart money' is just as stupid as everyone else." Amen to that. As smart as you and I might be in one area or maybe two, we are likely to be clueless in many others. I've been humbled enough times to admit that I have my own blind spots—and I've relied on other entrepreneurs to help shine a light on them. I sincerely hope this book will help you do the same, no matter where you are on your journey as an entrepreneur.

Note

1. Neil Patel, "90% of Startups Fail: Here's What You Need to Know About the 10%," Forbes.com, January 16, 2015.

Self-Assessment

That degree in business or finance or accounting definitely looks good on your résumé. You've also got an MBA? Well done. You're probably qualified for a job at a great company.

If you're looking to build a company from scratch, however, you'll need a lot more than book smarts. In fact, being too thoughtful or analytical is likely to keep you from making the fast decisions that are required to keep a new company afloat. But if you hate your job or your boss, don't fit in, or can't compete with your peers because of a learning disability—if you have this idea for a business but your friends and family think you're crazy to pursue it—congratulations. You might have what it takes to be a successful entrepreneur. But before you make your move, you must look deep into your character and gauge whether you can really juggle an endless number of competing demands and are armed with the traits that mark the successful entrepreneur, a whole other species of businessperson. Some of you will have no other choice than to give it a go.

LESSON 1

Know Thyself!

Young people often ask me, "What should I do?" Many of us have been there, just out of college or business school, searching for a job or trying to make a decision about a career. If you're lucky, you have some options. You wonder, "Should I take this job or that one?" Or maybe you think, "I just got an offer for a high-paying job in a major corporation, but I also have a great idea for a business. What should I do?"

These questions are posed as if one alternative might be better than the other on some objective scale. But nothing could be more subjective. It depends entirely on who's asking the question. What's your personality? How strong is your drive? How much grit and determination do you have? Do you crave individuality? Success? The only possible answer is: *Know thyself.*

Has there ever been advice so ancient, so well known, and so *ignored*? "Know thyself" was already a common maxim in the fourth century B.C., when it was emblazoned on the entrance to the Temple of Apollo in Delphi, home of the Delphic Oracle. In several of Plato's dialogues, Socrates notes the importance of this wisdom to living a virtuous life. And it's just as relevant today as it was back then.

I realized the importance of self-awareness as I grew older and was transitioning from one career to another. By my midtwenties, I had ruled out working for the government or a large corporation. I had nothing against either type of institution; my problem was more personal.

I am about as proud of my father as any son I know. Richard Sonnenfeldt lived an extraordinary life by any measure. Born in Germany, his parents sent him and his younger brother to a boarding school in England when he

11

was 16. It was 1938, and the decision was part of a plan to move the family from Nazi Germany. One year later, World War II was under way. England declared him, as it did all German refugees 16 and older, an "enemy alien." He was deported to an Australian internment camp. But it didn't take him long to convince his English captors that he was a Jewish refugee who wanted to fight Nazis—not be imprisoned with them.

On the trip back to England, his ship was torpedoed off the coast of India. As a 17-year-old refugee, he spent the next six months working as a manager of a radio factory in Bombay. In May 1941, he arrived in the United States, his fourth continent in three years. There, he was reunited with his parents, who had escaped from Germany and settled in Baltimore. Two years later, he enlisted in the army (receiving automatic citizenship for doing so), getting his chance to fight Nazis at the Battle of the Bulge and helping to liberate the Dachau concentration camp. In mid-1945, General Bill Donovan, the head of the Office of Strategic Services (OSS) and eventual founder of the CIA, selected him as an interpreter for the Nuremberg war crimes trials. He quickly rose, at the age of 23, to become the chief interpreter for the American prosecution. My father and a British major went from cell to cell to personally deliver the indictments to the 21 principal defendants at the first and most famous Nuremberg trial. He became the personal interpreter for Hermann Göring, the second in command of the German Third Reich.

Despite his extensive wartime experience, my father had yet to graduate from high school. Returning to Baltimore, he was directly admitted to the Johns Hopkins School of Engineering, from which he graduated in record time. Years later, he became the Distinguished Alumnus of the class of 1949. He held the final patents on color TV, which he designed while a young engineer at RCA, invented a circuit used in all radar detectors in the free world since 1951, and led the team that sent the first NASA satellite into space. And later in his career, he was dean of a business school too.

I can't imagine a better set of genes to have inherited. Guided by his amazing intuition, he trained me from an early age to have the confidence that I could achieve almost anything if I put my mind to it. Unfortunately, my father's capacious mind and amazing talent came with an emotional inflexibility and intolerance that took a toll on me as a child. It was only after years of analysis that I realized how much our relationship affected my becoming an entrepreneur. Being told what to do, when, and how would always remind me of some of my father's worst qualities, and I would instinctively resist. I guess I should be grateful for his less-than-ideal traits because they led me to entrepreneurship. I could not have achieved a fraction of the success I have if I were someone else's employee.

While I was writing this book, Marvin Israelow, my brother-in-law and an expert organizational consultant, reminded me of the work of Edgar Schein. Schein is a legendary MIT professor with whom Marvin worked in the late 1970s. One of the founders of the field of organizational psychology, Schein, now 88, is also famous for developing "a pattern of self-perceived talents, motives, and values" that organizes a person's work life and career ambitions, which he labeled "career anchors."[1]

Schein's original five career anchors, derived from a study of business school graduates 10 to 12 years into their various careers, were:

1. Technical/functional competence
2. Managerial competence
3. Security/stability
4. Autonomy/independence
5. Entrepreneurial creativity

He later added three more anchors:

6. Service or dedication to a cause
7. Pure challenge
8. Lifestyle

Marvin pointed out the two values that anchored my career and also appear as common denominators in the success stories of many of the entrepreneurs featured in this book: autonomy, which was significantly a reaction to my father's inflexibility, and creativity, which among Schein's entrepreneurs was expressed as "an overarching need to build or create something that was entirely their own product."

The real question for aspiring entrepreneurs isn't about what job you should take. It's about which job you are cut out for. It's about *you*—your capabilities, your weaknesses, your strengths, and, critically, your emotional sensitivities. If, like me, you can't stomach the idea of submitting yourself to the whims of an inflexible boss or a rigid institution—if the only way you can get satisfaction from a career is to create your own company—then entrepreneurship might make sense for you. But if you need a regular paycheck or your tolerance for risk is low, your career anchor is likely to be security/stability, number 3 on Schein's list. In that case, I would advise you to forget about starting your own business.

Determining if the entrepreneur's life is right for you takes self-reflection. It might surprise some people, but true self-reflection is the opposite of narcissism or self-absorption. And it's no easy task. It's undeniable that self-deception is part of what it is to be human. Psychotherapy was invented to get behind the mask we present not only to the world but also to ourselves. But it isn't the only path to genuine self-reflection.

Schein devised a "career anchor self-assessment" to help people manage their career choices. It involves a series of questions that can reveal the kind of work that is likely to satisfy you and your ambitions. Popular among managers and human resources professionals for evaluating prospective employees, Schein's self-assessment tool has been refined over the years and is now available both in book form and online.

As painful as self-knowledge is, it has a huge upside: Once you recognize your weaknesses, you will also better understand your strengths.

What is your definition of success? To answer that question, you have to step back—at every stage of your career—and make an effort to know thyself. I believe that the following lessons will help you in that never-ending quest.

Note

1. Edgar Schein, *Career Anchors* (San Diego: University Associates, 1985).

Self-Control Beats Passion

For the past few years, the average American savings rate has been about 5 percent, which lags far behind Europe's 10 percent and Japan's 40 percent. Still, it's an improvement, considering that in 2005 Americans saved just 1.9 percent, a record low. Bear in mind that those statistics do not include stock holdings, so if Bill Gates, for example, holds most of his wealth in Microsoft stock, he could be deemed a low saver. But even taking stock holdings into account, it's impossible to deny that Americans are comparatively poor savers. Twenty-four percent of us owe more money on our credit cards than we have in emergency savings. One-fifth of us don't even have savings accounts, and more than a third of American adults have not begun saving for retirement.

Why can't we show more self-control? For the past 40 years, an increasing number of behavioral economists have argued that most people do not act like the rational agents who populate economics textbooks. Instead of optimizing their personal and business goals, they do things that behavioral economist Dan Ariely describes as "predictably irrational."[1] Entrepreneurs, as you will see, have their own foibles, but excessive spending on ourselves is not one of them. This was brought home to me when I was in my twenties and working 80-hour weeks to grow my first business, while many of my peers in normal job situations were spending their evenings working on their social lives.

15

Most successful entrepreneurs either learn or are born with the capacity to delay gratification for critical periods in their lives. I've seen that capacity for self-control in many entrepreneurs who, even after their businesses became successful and even after they sold them for more than they could have imagined, continued to live simply and relatively modestly. It was this discipline that allowed them to plow their profits back into their businesses and maximize growth over the long term.

A lot of what we know about self-control comes from an ingenious experiment that the Stanford psychologist Walter Mischel created in 1968. Mischel wondered why a rational decision to delay his own gratification (vowing to pass on dessert in restaurants) so often lost its force in the face of a momentary temptation (the arrival of the pastry cart). To find out more, he used the Bing Nursery School at Stanford as a laboratory. Isolating each child in a room, he offered them a choice. They could receive one reward, such as a marshmallow, immediately, or they could wait 20 minutes (a lifetime for a four-year-old) and receive two rewards. Many couldn't last a minute, but a few were extremely creative at finding ways to distract themselves for the full 20 minutes.[2]

Over the next 40 years, Mischel and his grad students followed the 550 kids who had participated in the "Marshmallow Test," as the media nicknamed it, collecting information on their careers, marriages, and physical, financial, and mental health.[3] "The findings surprised us at the start, and they still do," wrote Mischel.[4] Not only were the preschoolers who were able to wait longer more focused, confident, and self-controlled as adolescents (the period when kids are most inclined to be out of control), but they also scored 210 points higher on their SAT tests.[5] To make sure that those results were not directed by the overall social environment of 1960s and 1970s California, the researchers replicated the experiments in different socioeconomic and geographic populations. The results were similar.[6]

What is particularly interesting is that the results seemed to correlate more with an individual's innate personality than with their intelligence. Research conducted by Angela Duckworth at the University of Pennsylvania's Center for Positive Psychology also bears this out. A former seventh-grade teacher, Duckworth decided to pursue a PhD in psychology to understand why it was that so many of her best-performing students were not those with the highest IQs. She has found that a student's self-control predicts report card grades better than measured intelligence. Outside the classroom, the Duckworth lab has shown that stronger self-control plays a role in lower levels of smoking, marijuana use, and binge drinking, and correlates with lifetime earnings, savings, and reported levels of life satisfaction.[7]

Is self-control a matter of genetic luck, or can it be taught? The latest research indicates that though we are all biologically prewired, nature is not as separable from nurture as was once presumed. While our natural dispositions tend to be more plastic in childhood, psychologists are learning that we can also change later in life by adopting more of an "I think I can" mindset. All of us will face momentary temptations that can distract us from our long-term goals. Mischel's recent research shows that our capacity to deal with them depends on our ability to bring the distant consequences of our actions to the present to undermine the appeal of a given temptation.[8] (For example: *If I eat too much, I may become obese. If I smoke, I may get lung cancer.*)

I would add: *If I don't focus on growing my business, it will fail.* I think it's time for psychologists to study the one segment of the American adult population that is full of maestros of self-control: successful entrepreneurs. When you ask successful entrepreneurs where their self-control comes from, they're likely to answer with their own questions: How else do you start a business and keep it afloat? How else could we compete or succeed? How do you power through the tough times to get to the successful times?

One of the reasons that so many entrepreneurs who are successful right out of the gate lose steam is that they can't resist the temptation to broadcast or just enjoy the fruits of their success. A seasoned entrepreneur himself, and a principal in a company that finances other businesses, George Heisel has witnessed this problem often:

> A couple has saved $200,000 to $300,000 between them, and they start a business, a diner, say. They use their life savings to advertise, spending $100,000 the first year. The diner grows, and it starts generating $150,000 in cash flow. They want to show how successful their new diner is, so they buy a Mercedes or a new house. Then the mortgage or car payments start, and soon they're no longer doing the same amount of advertising as last year, and they can't grow their business. And that's why they fail, because someone else with more cash to invest will open a diner nearby.[9]

Heisel resisted that temptation in 2001 when he started his own business, a medical supply company specializing in products for people with diabetes. For the first two years, he took no salary, plowing all his profits into advertising; as the business grew, he took only a small salary and made no distributions for seven years. He and his wife, a doctor, rented a house. It's a common story among successful founders, many of who start their businesses with savings: They funneled their earnings back into the business while also squirreling away as much cash as possible for a rainy day.

Delaying gratification is only one of the many attributes you'll need to succeed as an entrepreneur, as we'll see in the next several lessons.

Notes

1. Dan Ariely, *Predictably Irrational* (New York: HarperCollins, 2008).
2. Walter Mischel, *The Marshmallow Test: Mastering Self-Control* (New York: Little, Brown, 2014), 4–5.
3. Michael Shermer, "Book Review: 'The Marshmallow Test' by Walter Mischel," *Wall Street Journal* (September 19, 2014), https://www.wsj.com/articles/book-review-the-marshmallow-test-by-walter-mischel-1411160813.
4. Mischel, *The Marshmallow Test*, 23.
5. Ibid., 25.
6. Ibid.
7. Angela Lee Duckworth, "Grit: The Power of Passion and Perseverance," TED Talks Education (April 2013).
8. Mischel, *The Marshmallow Test*, 33–37.
9. George Heisel, interview (July 14, 2015).

LESSON 3

Be Wildly Optimistic — Delusional, Even

In 1986, Will Ade was enjoying his dream job as an explorations manager for a Texas-based oil company. Over the previous three years, he had identified a number of prospects—potential oil reservoirs—in Brunei that turned into major discoveries, and then more in Colombia that were drilled by Sun, BP, and Exxon. He was following this up by scouting in Indonesia. Will had proven his knack for finding oil and gas during an eight-year stint at Phillips Petroleum. He had worked his way through grad school as a field geologist in California and other western states and then became a full-time petroleum geophysicist involved in major ventures in the Philippines and Singapore. "My wells got drilled," he recalls.[1]

But big corporations move slowly. Eager to get his prospects drilled faster, Will had jumped to that smaller Texas firm. After enjoying those three years of success, he learned the downside of working for a small, undercapitalized company. Oil prices plunged 67 percent. Suddenly, Will was stuck in Indonesia without a job—and no severance. He and his wife had three kids in diapers and not much of a plan. "All we had were return tickets to the U.S., worth about $3,000."

But Will had one other crucial possession: unbridled optimism. Among the many things Will had learned in Asia was that "the Chinese pictogram for 'crisis' is the same as the one for 'opportunity.'" Yes, he had lost his job, but he still had his knack for finding oil and was tired of depending on someone else's decisions. So he cashed in the airline tickets and started his own wildcat exploration consultancy, based in Singapore.

19

Every would-be entrepreneur has a dream for a business. The best entrepreneurs *believe* they can make it happen, again and again. They just keep climbing from venture to venture, and if one ladder fails, they leap to another. To most people who work for a living, such optimism is abnormal. And they're right. *Normal* people do not risk their last $3,000 on a startup. What fuels that kind of risk taking is optimism of a very high level.

Daniel Kahneman, one of the world's most influential psychologists, found that kind of optimism to be so unsettling that he called it "entrepreneurial delusion."[2] Kahneman has spent his 40-year academic career studying how humans make decisions, and for the most part, he has not been impressed. The ingenious experiments that he designed—initially with his colleague Amos Tversky, who died in 1996—spurred the growth of the new field of behavioral economics. Their work earned Kahneman the Nobel Prize in economics in 2002. (Tversky was not similarly honored only because Nobel Prizes are not awarded posthumously.)

Overconfidence is so widespread among CEOs, investment advisors, journalists, academics, government officials, and other professional prognosticators that Kahneman and Tversky coined the phrase "planning fallacy" to account for the kinds of massive budget overruns that are endemic to so many projects.[3] Anyone who has undertaken a major home renovation is likely to have also been a victim of the planning fallacy. A 2002 survey of American homeowners who had remodeled their kitchens found that, on average, the actual cost exceeded the budget by more than 100 percent!

Research shows that this optimistic bias tends to be highest among entrepreneurs and inventors, leading them to indulge in what Kahneman calls "fast thinking." *Fast thinking* is going with your gut,[4] and this propensity commits entrepreneurs to ventures that are too risky and costly. For Kahneman, the world would be a much better place if we all worked harder at being slower thinkers, relying less on intuition and emotion and more on focused, deliberative logic.

To be fair, Kahneman ends up quite ambivalent about the role optimism plays in American life. He concedes that the growing body of research indicates that "if you were allowed one wish for your child, seriously consider wishing him or her optimism."[5] Optimists tend to be cheerful, happy, and popular. They are likely to have stronger immune systems and thus better health. They are more resilient and bounce back from failure. Optimists even live longer than their less hopeful compatriots. Kahneman also admits that optimism is "the engine of capitalism," stating: "When action is needed, optimism, even of the mildly delusional variety, may be a good thing."[6]

Although Kahneman acknowledges the importance of optimism to personal and business success, he seems irked by the fact that these very successful people have also been very lucky in life—and typically do not acknowledge it. I will plead guilty to that charge. Early in my career as an entrepreneur, I was more inclined to attribute my initial success to my skills than I would today. But mine was hardly a rags-to-riches story. My father was a brilliant engineer and an executive vice president at NBC. I went to great schools, got a plum job at a leading firm, and worked for a few years at my wife's family's real estate company. I had more opportunities in my early twenties than many people see over the course of their entire career.

But that was 35 years ago, and I'm still creating new companies. Yes, luck is important, and I'm quite realistic about where I stand on the scale between those who pulled a rabbit out of a hat and the true geniuses among us. But I'm still not sure that Kahneman hasn't overstated the role of luck. If Kahneman were to meet Will Ade or hundreds of our other Tiger 21 members, he would soon find out that their high levels of optimism are fueled by an equally impressive capacity for *slow thinking*.

While Will Ade cashed in his family's airline tickets to start his company, that wasn't simply an act of foolish optimism. He was a highly trained geologist and geophysicist with a world-class record of finding drillable oil reserves. He also knew that his infant company with its minimal overhead would be able to underbid the competition. What about employees to carry out the exploration contracts? Will, who'd earned an MBA while working for Phillips, had that covered. He was not the only experienced oil and gas man stuck in Southeast Asia without a job. "I hired all my buddies who had been laid off," he recalls with a chuckle.

It turned out Will also had a knack for entrepreneurship. His company proceeded to generate new ventures as well as mergers and acquisitions for publicly held companies and private investors. Over the next three decades, he confirmed his ability for slow thinking again and again, exploring for oil and gas reserves in Brunei, Singapore, Malaysia, the Philippines, and Vietnam, while also investing in farms, ranches, and forests in his native Indiana. Will currently holds overriding royalty interests in several of his discoveries in Southeast Asia and continues to be involved in new ventures and exploration prospects for select clients. His net worth today: nine figures and growing.

Some might read this and think, "That dude just got really lucky." The controversy over the role of luck in business and investing always reminds me of a famous speech Warren Buffett gave in 1984. In it he defended the "value investing" approach that he learned from his Columbia Business School mentors, Benjamin Graham and David Dodd, whose classic book, *Security*

Analysis, had been published 50 years earlier. "The professors who write textbooks," he argued, were wrong to claim that the Graham-Dodd system was outdated because the efficient market thoroughly researches companies and prices them accordingly, leaving no undervalued equities. According to that point of view, investors who beat the market were simply lucky.[7]

Buffett pointed to a group of eight extremely successful investors (which included himself and his partner, Charlie Munger) who had used the Graham-Dodd system to beat the S&P 500 Index by significant margins for decades. To illustrate how such an extraordinary correlation had to involve more than luck, Buffett asked his audience to imagine that 225 million Americans (roughly the entire U.S. population at the time) agreed to participate in a national coin-flipping contest. The contest begins with every American betting a dollar on the flip of a coin. The losers drop out, and each subsequent day, the winners bet their cumulative winnings on a daily coin toss. The losers keep dropping out and the winners, the ranks of which are cut in half each day, have twice as much each day to bet.

After 20 days, there would be 215 people left who had won every single day. All of that would be due to pure chance, Buffet conceded. Had 225 million orangutans flipped coins, the results would have been identical. However, pure luck would probably distribute the 215 winning apes evenly around the country. If you instead "found out that 40 came from a particular zoo in Omaha," Buffett noted, "you'd be pretty sure you were on to something." You would then start looking for patterns of possible causes other than coincidence, just as scientists would if a rare cancer appeared in an unusual number of citizens in a particular mining town. Buffett concluded that the disciplines he and the other Graham-Dodd adherents used to beat the S&P for decades was proof that "a disproportionate number of successful coin flippers in the investment world came from a very small intellectual village that could be called Graham-and-Doddsville."

Buffett's speech explains that successful investing takes more than luck, and the same goes for entrepreneurship. Most of the successful entrepreneurs I know come from a place that nurtured their self-control, grit, and optimism. They were lucky too, but I have learned that luck tends to favor those who are prepared and willing to take the risk when the right opportunity comes along.

Notes

1. Will Ade, interviews (February 19 and August 14, 2015).
2. Daniel Kahneman, *Thinking, Fast and Slow* (New York: Farrar, Straus and Giroux, 2011), 256.

3. Daniel Kahneman and Amos Tversky, "Intuitive Prediction: Biases and Corrective Procedures," *Forecasting: Methods and Applications*, 2nd ed. by Spyros G. Makridakis and Steven C. Wheelwright (New York: John Wiley & Sons, 1983), 313–27.

4. Kahneman, *Thinking*. See Note 1.

5. Ibid., 255.

6. Ibid., 256.

7. Warren Buffett, "The Superinvestors of Graham-and-Doddsville" (speech, Columbia Business School, May 17, 1984), https://www8.gsb.columbia.edu/rtfiles/cbs/hermes/Buffett1984.pdf.

Let Others Underestimate You

I don't know a single entrepreneur who hasn't heard a version of the following message: *You can't do it. It'll never happen.*

To overcome the skeptics and the naysayers, nearly all entrepreneurs need grit and a level of optimism that can seem delusional, as Will Ade's story (Lesson 3) so powerfully illustrates.

Female entrepreneurs especially require superhuman levels of these traits. It's tough for anyone to build a company out of nothing more than an idea, but I have found that all too frequently the female entrepreneurs I know have been underestimated in such a pathological way that the only word that can accurately describe it is *sexism.*

One of the opportunities that writing a book like this provides is the experience of hearing other people's stories. I thought I knew many of the ins and outs of what it takes to be a successful entrepreneur, but listening to the stories of female entrepreneurs allowed me to more fully appreciate the fact that sexism is an additional challenge so many successful women have had to overcome.

The most consistent and disturbing pattern I witnessed was that many women wanted to revise the stories they had told me after they saw their words in a printed draft. In the quiet of an initial interview, many women shared stories of bosses or clients pressuring them for sex, male colleagues forcing them to attend work events held at strip clubs, or simply the consistent onslaught of sexual innuendo they endured over the years. Initially, these women wanted to share the challenges they faced so that young readers, especially women facing similar obstacles, might be inspired to persevere. However, when they finally saw their story in print, they often wanted key details removed because they didn't want to be perceived as victims—or because they didn't want to harm the men who had behaved so poorly toward them. I'm not sure I'd have the same restraint.

The key insights for me are how much abuse women in the workplace face, how much they have learned to grin and bear it, and how few men understand how insidious this is. I didn't.

But the data certainly supports their stories. In 2015, the Global Entrepreneurship Monitor, the largest and longest study on entrepreneurship around the world, put out a special report on female entrepreneurship. It found that men are still 50 percent more likely to become entrepreneurs. It's not that women don't see business opportunities—they do. The problem is that they don't see themselves as capable of pulling off success, and they have a greater fear of failure than men who see the same opportunities. (Perhaps women are actually more realistic.) In the United States, 61 percent of men said they believed they could successfully start a business compared to only 46 percent of women surveyed.

Should it really come as a surprise that would-be women entrepreneurs systemically underestimate themselves? After all, when we consider the most successful entrepreneurs on the planet today, nearly all their names are male: Bill, Sergey, Warren, Mark, Larry . . . you get the picture.

The Global Entrepreneurship Monitor has found that only 15 percent of companies that get venture capital funding have a woman on their executive team. For companies with a female CEO, the number drops to 3 percent. And yet, there are women who have powerfully defied these odds. What I have found most fascinating about their journeys is that they all used the fact they were being underestimated to their advantage.

Take the story of Joan Price. Joan's path was fraught with difficulty from the beginning. Her mother suffered from chronic illness, and Joan moved to Israel when she was only 15. At her new Israeli high school, she had to repeat the 10th and 11th grades. As an ideological stance against capitalism, her socialist high school did not offer diplomas, so despite her extra years in school, Joan never got a diploma!

Thanks to her determination, her quest for learning, and a simple bureaucratic error, Joan managed to get into Tel Aviv University, where she studied economics. "I ended up going in through the back door to almost everything in life," Joan says. "I have not lived a life of entitlement. No one ever made a call to get me into Harvard."[1]

Eventually, Joan married, had kids, and completed a master's degree in finance. She then returned to New York permanently to care for her ailing mother. Her mother's sole source of income was a building that she owned in Chelsea. "Back then [in the 1980s]," remembers Joan, "the neighborhood was nothing like it is today. The meatpacking district right next door was a red-light district, full of hookers. Chelsea wasn't much better."

Joan was eager to get into the real estate business and was able to stop her mother from selling that single building. "The minute I took over, I started looking around for a second building." In 1986, that second building revealed itself: a small, four-unit building in the West Village that cost $750,000. Joan only had $100,000 to invest. It was certainly not enough for a down payment. Her sister stepped up to the plate and offered an additional $100,000. They became equal partners.

That building was just the beginning. "I kept on acquiring buildings—small ones at first because I didn't have money," Joan says. Where other buyers saw dilapidation, she saw opportunity. "I take the most god-awful slums you ever saw, and I buy those black holes and turn them around."

Today, Joan owns dozens of buildings in New York and has become a known operator. "I made us into a real estate family." She did it despite the fact that no one believed she could do it. "Everyone dismissed me and treated me as invisible," she says.

Part of it may have to do with her own initial self-presentation: "I had my mom's self-deprecating invisibility. I looked and acted like a nobody," she says. Being a woman in a male-dominated business made her even easier to overlook. "There are women in real estate, of course, but no one does what I do. I am willing to take on challenges to unlock value very few others would dare to risk. The fact that I am a woman makes it all the more unusual."

Being underestimated often helped her slip under her competitors' radar. All too often, sellers let their guard down because Joan was the only one showing such interest; they didn't realize how much upside there might be.

Like Joan, Eva Losacco had to fend for herself from an early age. Her parents were both Yugoslavian immigrants; her dad was a janitor, and her mom worked in a tent factory. Neither spoke English, so at seven years old, Eva began to become independent when she was sent out to find a Catholic school for herself and her brother.

The family lived in a one-bedroom apartment. Eva, her younger brother, and her grandmother shared the bedroom, and her parents slept in a Murphy bed in the living room. Their Chicago neighborhood was rough. One time, a juvenile delinquent smashed Eva's head into a brick wall.

Despite their dreary circumstances, Eva's parents provided a remarkable example of working hard for a better life, and she never felt that she was missing anything. She had jobs from the time she was 11 years old—something she views as a gift. "It made me so independent. It made me feel competent."[2] She also excelled in school, especially in science. In the eighth grade, she won a local science fair, which earned her a spot in the regionals. She won that too and eventually headed to the state science fair. Eva won the prize—and with it a scholarship to an all-girls Catholic high school.

Growing up watching her parents work so hard for little money made her own goals clear. "It was all about the money and the focus," she says. "I never let anything derail me."

Plenty of men tried. Early in her career, Eva worked at a company that sold components for off-highway equipment and the aerospace industry. Sexism was the norm. Her engineering coworkers would take her to restaurants that, conveniently, had lingerie shows along with lunch. "It was bizarre," she admits. But she put on a smile and never let on that she was uncomfortable. "I was never going to let them see me squirm."

That sort of lurking sexism would prove to be a recurring theme in Eva's career. A decade later, at another job, the head of the company told her during her initial interview, "I can't hire a woman. What if you're in the middle of a big deal and you have to go home and make dinner for your husband?" Eva's response? "You're not going to have that problem. I would never marry a man incapable of making himself a sandwich."

That boss never did change—"He was like Donald Trump on steroids"—but Eva forged past his indiscretions. Knowing that being a woman in the high-growth but male-dominated tech and finance fields would hold her back from getting high salaries and top jobs, Eva made sure to use it to her advantage. "I always made sure that I chose performance-based payment structures. Getting paid on commission allowed me to prove myself, and it was always totally clear what value I added." Soon, she was the top-paid person in the whole company.

Money doesn't lie. And her boss couldn't dispute the fact that Eva was a killer salesperson who ultimately helped grow the company into a $700 million enterprise.

"I chose to not take any of it personally or let it get to me," Eva says of such experiences. Instead, she worked around the sexists and kept a single-minded focus on her own goals. It was a feminist strategy of a very pragmatic sort: "Here's an obstacle. How do I get around it?"

At one company where Eva worked, she was the top sales rep when she became pregnant. She expected to receive $75,000 in pay during her six-week maternity leave. The official company policy was that women on maternity leave would receive a percentage of their prior-year salary in compensation. But the head of human resources called her to tell her that the company was going to pay her only $17,000. Eva admits she considered suing, but she realized, "It would just hurt me more and could damage my reputation and chance for a better job. Better to keep my eye on the prize." Ultimately, she chose to leave rather than sue, which resulted in much better opportunities and greater financial rewards.

Today Eva is successful beyond her wildest expectations, and perhaps most impressively, she is able to shrug off the misogynists who tried to get in her way.

Most entrepreneurs who make it are exceptional, but women like Joan and Eva are all the more so. The obstacles they encountered weren't just about the market, but about their gender. These two women have grit—a quality that, as we'll see in the next lesson, is perhaps the most important predictor of an entrepreneur's success.

Notes

1. Joan Price, interview (February 3, 2017).
2. Eva Losacco, interview (February 3, 2017).

Grit Beats IQ—Most of the Time

Optimism fuels the entrepreneur's journey past the naysayers. Self-control is a psychological mechanism for beating off temptations that seem irresistible, at least at the moment. But given the high failure rate for startups, successful entrepreneurs typically struggle for a decade or more to build a business that just might eventually appeal to a buyer. To keep struggling requires an additional psychological trait: grit. Angela Duckworth and her colleague James Gross define grit as "having and working assiduously toward a single challenging superordinate goal through thick and thin, on a timescale of years or even decades."[1]

Duckworth's research into the psychological factors affecting achievement has enabled her to predict which teachers and students will succeed in tough inner-city public schools, who will survive the notorious cadet summer training before the first term at West Point, and which candidates will ultimately make it into the U.S. Army's Special Forces, regardless of IQ, standardized test scores, or even physical fitness.[2]

Duckworth has not studied entrepreneurs, but her definition of grit pretty much summarizes most of the successful entrepreneurs I've listened to over the past two decades. Almost every one of them has faced moments of crisis when the businesses they were building suddenly cratered. Each of them coolly reviewed the situation, came up with a plan of attack, pressed their grit buttons, and spent the next several years revamping their operations into enterprises valued at tens of millions of dollars and more.

31

Take Ed Doherty, for example.[3] Ed was born in Brooklyn and raised by a single mother who worked as a housekeeper and bookkeeper until she'd saved enough money to buy a deli on Long Island. Ed worked there for 40 hours a week during high school and college and 60 hours a week during the summer.

By 1973, Ed was working in the real estate division of Burger King, selecting sites for new restaurants on the East Coast, when he got a call from Marriott, which was looking for someone to do the same for their fast-food restaurants. "You have a good reputation," said the man from Marriott, offering him $25,000 a year. Ed was already making $24,000, so he figured he was in a position to make a counterproposal: $26,000. "If he said yes, I'd take the job. If he said no, I'd stay with Burger King," he recalled.

Ed got his bump in salary. During the next five years, he became a maestro of site selection and was promoted to the number-two position in Marriott's restaurant real estate division. He soon requested a transfer to operations, where he ran a third of the Roy Rogers restaurants in the New York metro area. Then, in 1984, he took an even bigger step up the corporate ladder when he was promoted to general manager and vice president in Marriott's Washington, DC, headquarters, running Big Boy Restaurants of America, which had 1,200 locations. He and his wife, Joan, who had just given birth to their third child, found a house they liked in the DC area.

While his wife was preparing for the move, Ed started working at headquarters and quickly realized that his talent as a manager would do him no good in a culture where some executives tried to win favor by sabotaging others. Ed was making more money than he had ever dreamed of. Even so, he called Joan in New Jersey and told her to put the move on hold. "We've got to figure something out."

In fact, Ed already had figured it out. He wanted to buy the 19 Roy Rogers restaurants that had been his responsibility before his promotion. They each averaged $640,000 in total annual sales and lost $700,000. "I thought I could turn them around." He persuaded Marriott CEO, Richard Marriott, to sell him the restaurants for a million dollars and quickly found a bank that would give him a personal loan for the money. Then he and his wife had the hardest conversation of all. "I said to her," Ed recalls, 'Okay, honey, I'm going to give up this job making $200,000, we have a mortgage on the house, and I'm going to borrow a million dollars personally. And we won't have a salary for a period of time. But this is an opportunity to control our destiny.'" Fortunately, she gave him the green light.

Over the next five years, Ed's new regime doubled the restaurants' annual average sales. He borrowed more money to add another nine Roy Rogers franchises to his stable and then made a deal with TJ Cinnamons to buy six bakery cafés. "Life was good," recalls Ed.

Then, it was not so good. In 1990, as part of a long-term strategic plan, Marriott decided to exit the fast-food restaurant business, selling its Big Boy and Roy Rogers operations to Hardee's. In Ed's opinion, the new owners "destroyed the Roy Rogers brand" over the next three years. Ed owed $4.5 million to banks and "saw it all going down the tubes." And then he did what every successful entrepreneur I know does when hitting a wall. "I didn't blame myself," Ed explains. "I didn't blame anybody. I just said, 'I've got a problem. I've got to develop a plan, work the plan, and if it's the right plan, I will come out of this successfully.'" In other words, he pushed his grit button.

He asked his bank to restructure his loan, but they refused because they only take that step once borrowers are delinquent. Ed quickly solved that problem because he had no choice but to stop making his loan payments. As he was nearly out of money, the decision was easy. He also had to stop paying royalties to Hardee's. "I couldn't afford to pay the loans and the royalties *and* my employees," he explains. "My people come first." He then hired the best lawyers he could find to help him renegotiate deals with Hardee's and his bankers, which he was able to do without declaring bankruptcy.

Over the next few years, Ed continued to sell his leases while persuading the bank to reduce his loan to $3 million and convincing Hardee's to forgive his royalty payments. In less than a year he had the $3 million to pay off the loan, which wasn't even due for another four years. Proving to be a very persuasive fellow, Ed talked the bank into reducing the loan by another $700,000. "Cash is better than waiting for something," he rationalized.

With enough money to stay in business, most owners would have stuck to their knitting. Ed, however, began looking for his next opportunity. He liked the Applebee's brand, which was expanding in the east. The company resisted. Ed didn't have the net worth to qualify as an Applebee's franchisee. But he persisted: "Isn't there some way we can work around this?"

The company agreed to work with him, and Ed opened his first two Applebee's restaurants in New Jersey in 1993. Meanwhile, he was selling off his Roy Rogers locations, paying off his bank loan—and looking for more opportunities. He found six locations that he thought would work for Wendy's. He contacted the Wendy's corporate office to ask about converting his existing Roy Rogers restaurants. He wondered if they would lend him the money because his bank wouldn't. Wendy's agreed, mainly because they were already considering buying 150 Roy Rogers New Jersey and Long Island locations from Hardee's and rebranding them as Wendy's. Ed had offered them a quick test case. He converted three of his Roy Rogers sites into Wendy's restaurants, and his sales tripled. In 1995, he built two more Applebee's restaurants and converted his three remaining Roy Rogers locations into Wendy's restaurants.

In three years, Ed had gone from the verge of bankruptcy to success. Six years later, he had 10 Wendy's franchises and valuable experience. He had learned that his success—and his family's future—depended in large part on the success of his franchiser. That didn't sit well with him, so he decided to sell his Wendy's restaurants in order "to put enough money in our pocket that our family would never have to worry again."

Ed, 69, is doing fine. The company he heads, Doherty Enterprises, now owns and operates 107 Applebee's restaurants, 43 Panera Bread cafes, and has also developed two Irish pubs and two wine bars. At the time I spoke to him in 2016, he expected yearly sales of $500 million. "It was all luck," says Ed with a shrug that has won the hearts, minds, and cash of many bankers.

That kind of hard-won *luck* is a common denominator in the careers of many members of Tiger 21, but occasionally we hear stories that move even the toughest among us. When Rick Bennett joined Tiger 21 and told his story to his fellow members in Austin, Texas, during one of his early meetings, he was welcomed as someone they knew quite well—the partner in a successful wealth management company who made money making look easy. Their perception changed, however, once Rick told the story of what it took to make his way into our network.[4]

Twenty years earlier, as Rick and his partner were starting their business, Rick's marriage fell apart. The divorce was messier than most and, as if that weren't enough to derail Rick from the single-minded focus and effort required in the early stages of any new business, he soon learned that his former wife would be unable to share in joint custody of their three young children. Rick would be a single parent.

He had to make a stark choice between the future of his new business and his children. He went to his business partner with his decision. "I take care of things. I don't drop things in my life, and I'm not going to drop the kids." They were his first priority; his health was his second. "If something gets dropped, it's going to be work. So we have to figure out a way that I can have some flexibility to go to school events and do what I need to do."

They worked it out, and Rick proceeded to do what he needed to do, which was to divide his life between building the business and taking care of his kids. For the next two decades, he pulled off an impressive balancing act, helping with their homework, having their friends over at his house, and traveling with them—all while advancing the company. He made a conscious choice to not remarry. He had some relationships, but he never brought anyone into the house.

When Rick told his story, "There was absolute silence in the room as the magnitude of the challenges he faced poured out," recalls Chris Ryan, who chairs the Austin chapter of Tiger 21. "The respect in that room for Rick—you could feel it."

Rick shrugs off those 20 years of resilience. "I didn't agonize over it or feel sorry for myself," he said, echoing Ed Doherty. "I just did it. I not only did it, I enjoyed it."

I suspect that one of the reasons Rick's story grabbed that room so tightly was that many of us were able to apply our customary grit only because we had an understanding, flexible significant other taking care of business at home. The other members were no doubt wondering whether they could have pulled it off as a single parent. Candice Carpenter Olson wouldn't have been wondering. She's another person who did it. Indeed, when I think about the grittiest entrepreneurs I know, Candice Carpenter Olson leaps to mind.

In the early 1990s, Candice was a highly ambitious, successful woman in Manhattan. She had already had an extremely impressive career in the corporate world. By the time she was 40, she'd been a vice president at American Express, the president of Time-Life Video, and the president of Q2, a high-end version of QVC that she built with Barry Diller. She gained a reputation for being tough enough to stand up to him, though she claims she felt like hiding under the desk most days.

She realized how desperate she was to be her own boss when, on the way to interviews with various corporations, she would get sick to her stomach and actually throw up. "There couldn't have been a clearer sign," she said. "I had to strike out on my own."[5]

At that time, the Internet was just beginning to emerge into the public consciousness, and Candice, who had been advising one of the top executives at AOL, saw a huge opportunity to create an online network targeted at women. As a single woman, Candice knew how hard it was to find the right partner. She was dating a lot, but she couldn't find anyone worth committing to.

"We were full of religious fervor about the idea," she says. But investors didn't get the concept at first. "They would look at me and say, 'Women won't ever use the Internet.'" It sounds laughable now, but at the time it was the conventional wisdom.

She tuned out the naysayers and forged ahead. In 1995, Candice founded iVillage. By 1999, the company was worth $2 billion.

While she was doing all this, Candice was also a single mother to a toddler. She had decided it was better to start a family on her own than to settle for the wrong partner. The fact that she was able to create a successful startup while she entered motherhood as a single parent is something that many people can't quite believe.

Candice knew that when an entrepreneur chooses the wrong mate, the results—both personal and professional—are disastrous. "Entrepreneurs are artists, and they need the emotional support an artist needs," she says. "A CEO is lonely. An entrepreneur CEO is even more lonely. But a female entrepreneur CEO with a kid? That was sort of one of a kind."

It was tough, she admits, but she found a way to make it work. She hired a student cook who would prepare dinner every night for her and her young daughter. "I'd go rushing home at six o'clock and skid into my seat at the dinner table. Then, I would spend a few hours with my daughter, completely present. The minute I put her to bed, asleep beside me, I would whip out my computer and work until midnight or later. It was very intense, but I wouldn't have done it any other way. Now my daughter is starting her first company at 22."

The coda to Candice's story is equally unexpected: Within two years of stepping down as CEO of iVillage in 2000, she met her husband, Peter, the head of Random House at the time. Together, their family has seven children, three adopted from Eastern Europe. Both Candice and Peter are currently working on new companies of their own.

I'm sure Candice would agree with Rick's assessment of pulling off entrepreneurship as a single parent: "If it were easy, everyone would be doing it." That's something that every entrepreneur struggling to grind it out should memorize.

Notes

1. Angela Duckworth and James J. Gross, "Self-Control and Grit: Related but Separable Determinants of Success," *Current Directions in Psychological Science* 23:5 (October 15, 2014), 319.

2. Angela Duckworth, *Grit: The Power of Passion and Perseverance* (New York: Scribner, 2016).

3. Ed Doherty, interview (July 16, 2015).

4. Rick Bennett, interview (September 8, 2015).

5. Candice Carpenter Olson, interview (February 3, 2017).

LESSON 6

Experience at a First-Rate Company Is Really Valuable

When I first heard this lesson, it struck me as so obviously true that I wanted to kick myself for not having thought of it first. I immediately flashed back to 1978, the year I spent at Goldman Sachs. Despite all the controversies that Goldman Sachs has been embroiled in recently, at the time, in my mind, it was the gold standard for a world-class organization. Goldman Sachs had the greatest collection of financial talent under a single umbrella.

I was recruited by the firm's mergers and acquisitions (M&A) department, the number one M&A shop on Wall Street that year. They hired just one associate: me. I was beyond thrilled. But when I walked through the door on my first day of work, I quickly noticed that I was the only professional sporting a beard and wearing Earth Shoes. (I bet you don't even remember Earth Shoes.) From day one I realized I was cut from a different cloth than my colleagues.

The co-leaders of our department were Geoff Boisi, Goldman's youngest partner at the time, and Steve Friedman, who would become Goldman's co-chariman with Robert Rubin (who served as Bill Clinton's treasury secretary). After Goldman, Steve went on to become head of the National Economic Council under George W. Bush, served on the Foreign Intelligence Advisory Board under Bill Clinton, and then chaired it under George W. Bush. Eventually he became chairman of the New York Federal Reserve Board.

I loved being surrounded by so many intense, ambitious, supersmart people. And I loved carrying a Goldman Sachs business card. We were all taking part in Goldman's team-building process, which de-emphasized individual egos. Co-chairs ran the firm and every department within it. This was unique, and the firm's emphasis on the value of partnership has colored my approach to almost every subsequent business relationship I have had.

But for all that, it didn't take me long to realize that my job was not exactly what I thought I had signed up for. It wasn't the long hours that I minded. (Everyone—by which I mean the junior staff—was expected to work from nine a.m. to midnight or later most days, plus weekends). Two things got to me. The first was my immediate supervisor, who acted like a jerk. The second was that the work felt too "ivory tower" for me. Until I got to Goldman, I hadn't realized that my real passion was for rolling up my shirtsleeves and doing whatever it took to grow a business. About three months into the job, I went to visit Friedman to get one-on-one advice. This took some courage. Friedman, a champion college wrestler, was not known for small talk.

I told him that I wasn't sure how well things were working out, and that I wasn't sure I was enjoying the experience. I was seeking guidance for how to fit in a little better. He listened to me intently and, to my shock, snapped, "Well, Sonnenfeldt, do you want to leave?" What happened next is seared indelibly into my memory forever. The next 30 seconds passed like a lifetime. I reviewed in my mind the downside of leaving. My mother was dying of cancer at the time, and I imagined a front-page *New York Times* headline, STUPID SONNENFELDT WALKS AWAY FROM CAREER OPPORTUNITY OF A LIFETIME!

But then, from somewhere deep within me, came the words, "Well, yes . . . I think I do." I was violating every rule of discipline and sanity my father had taught me. Without missing a beat, Friedman replied, "Well, we knew you were bright but different when we hired you. Is there any place else in the firm you would like to work?"

As coincidence would have it, literally that very morning, as I had headed to my office, the elevator had stopped on the floor below mine where a sign caught my eye. It read GOLDMAN SACHS REALTY CORP. "How about the real estate department?" I answered. Friedman picked up the phone and called the partner in charge, Shelley Seevak. The following Monday, I reported to Shelley.

Over the past four decades, I have often flashed back to Friedman's reaction that day. The way he listened to a very nervous kid and then quickly explored other beneficial options remains for me an example of the kind of intelligence and flexibility that a world-class firm breeds into their teams. Whenever I've been up against an organizational problem in my business career, I've thought, "How would the best people at Goldman Sachs have approached this issue?"

You will be less likely to get that particular kind of insight or experience if your first job is starting your own company. Smart and resilient people can learn from almost any experience, but many of the entrepreneurs I know have attributed much of their success to experience in an established and successful firm. As George Heisel, the medical supply company founder in Lesson 2, says, there's no substitute for "rolling up your sleeves and working six to seven days a week" in a well-run corporation. "You have to have a lot of experience to operate your own business successfully," George explains. "People get into businesses like mine, and they don't realize how much regulation they have to comply with. In my business, for example, I had to deal with at least six different government agencies, including the FCC, FDA, Medicaid, and the Department of Justice."[1]

When George started his company at 35, he had already logged more than 20 years in the health care industry. He began at age 12, working after school and over the summer for his family's ambulance company, which his grandfather had founded in Rochester, New York. After college, he joined the firm full time. Four years later, his father sold the company to Rural Metro Corp., which operated emergency medical services in cities across the United States and Latin America, and George stayed on as an employee. "I was at the very bottom of 18,000 employees in terms of salary and respect," he recalls. Rural Metro had purchased about 70 local mom-and-pop ambulance companies, and George's new corporate bosses assumed he was just another spoiled heir. On the contrary: "My father overworked me and underpaid me, and used to joke that I should pay him for the experience," George recalls. "I now think he was right."

Placed under the supervision of an up-and-coming senior vice president who worked seven days a week, George too worked 24/7, mastering the business. He was soon running Rural Metro's Phoenix operation. Three years later, when he was 30, he was general manager of the company's 911 service in San Diego; a year after that he was appointed a regional president in charge of 11 operations in Argentina, Brazil, and Bolivia, managing 3,500 employees.

"I don't think young people today understand how entrepreneurial you have to be to succeed in most corporations," George says. "It's just so hard to get things done that you have to be innovative; you have to make decisions; and you have to empower your team." George concedes that there were times when the bureaucratic wrangling drove him to the verge of quitting. But he soon realized that it was an experience of a lifetime. "I always dreamed of starting my own business, but without that corporate experience, I think the likelihood of success would have been diminished."

He advises working for a corporation "for at least 5 years but not more than 10. After 10 years, as a mentor of mine once explained, you become successful in an institution but not necessarily in the world." George watched a number of top executives in big companies based in Rochester try to make it as entrepreneurs. "These Kodak, Xerox, or Bausch & Lomb guys with big jobs and high salaries would leave thinking they were going to be the most successful business guys in the world, but they didn't have a clue about how to make payroll and manage cash—and failed." He also recommends working for a fast-growing corporation that is more likely to give younger people P&L responsibility. "With that kind of hands-on experience, you can envision what your own business should look like at 10 or 20 years out."

But don't despair if you've already spent more than a decade climbing the corporate ladder. Ed Doherty spent 25 years as an executive for three major U.S. corporations before he decided to take control of his destiny by buying 19 money-losing restaurants.

Another entrepreneur, who wishes to remain anonymous, we'll call Eleanor. Eleanor logged 20 quite happy, creative years in executive positions at media companies in Asia, Latin America, and the United States without a thought about starting her own business.[2] Then, an old friend, a medical doctor, asked her to partner in starting a health company for women, and Eleanor found herself leaning in. About a decade ago, the two women joined forces and founded their company. "It was a huge surprise. I loved having my own thing in a way that I never imagined I would," Eleanor recalls. "Someone I worked with not that long ago said to me, 'Have you always been this driven?' My answer was, 'No.'" While always an active and engaged corporate executive, running her own business lit a fire Eleanor had never known she had. She certainly had a lot to learn about the health care business, but her corporate experience added value to the partnership.

"The most important thing I ever learned in the corporate world was that if you are making someone accountable, they need the authority to make decisions. When you are starting up a company, it's 'all hands on deck,' and your core team has a voice in everything. It can get very muddy. But as you grow, you've got to create a structure where there is role clarity and clear accountability. Transitioning from a startup culture to a real business can be a huge hurdle if you don't know what this 'accountability and authority' looks like."

After a handful of offers, Eleanor and her partner sold their business to a private equity company that had already bought their major competitor. Eleanor's corporate experience and understanding of how companies run at scale made her the best candidate to run the combined company as it became a serious and established business. Just a few years after the two businesses were merged, the private equity owner decided to take the company to market with Eleanor as CEO. Among the prospective buyers were large, publicly traded companies in the same industry. Eleanor was concerned about the prospect of returning to corporate life. "I had found my passion—I was completely in the flow—and was afraid of losing it within a larger corporate structure. What was most important to me was keeping the fire alive and my team smart, agile, and entrepreneurial. I had learned so many important things from my corporate life, but I wanted to use those learnings to build something new, not spend my energy reintegrating into a new corporate culture with dynamics and rituals that may not best serve the business or my customers."

So last year, the company was sold to another private equity group instead—with Eleanor remaining as CEO. For this health care entrepreneur, her time in corporate America gave her a set of skills that helped her transition from having an idea to helping create a successful startup to leading an established but still independent business.

Notes

1. George Heisel, interview (July 14, 2015).
2. Anonymous, interview (July 31, 2015).

Your Disability Can Be an Advantage

For years I've reveled in knowing many brilliant entrepreneurs who have overcome some hole in their lives that made it difficult for them to succeed in structured environments like school, a corporation, or any large organization. These struggles include such challenges as an absent, abusive, or alcoholic parent; learning disabilities, such as dyslexia and attention deficit disorder (ADD); and even drug addiction. It seems that a disproportional number of successful entrepreneurs have faced these difficulties and succeeded in spite of them.

If such challenges have overshadowed your talents, you should know that you're already tougher than most of your peers; moreover, having something to prove can be a powerful motivator for growing a successful business. My father-in-law used to call it becoming a "broken field runner," the player who lets no obstacle get in his way. If one strategy fails, he quickly finds another path to the goal line.

"You know what the definition of an entrepreneur is? Thirty years old and just been fired," Rick Gornto tells me.[1] He ought to know. He spent his late twenties struggling, working in various jobs without ever feeling comfortable in a corporate structure, always too eager to go in his own direction. Applying for a position as a salesman, he was asked to take a test. "Two days later the guy sat me down and said, 'Son, I can't hire you. This test says you'll never make it as a salesman.'"

Rick was never a great test-taker, but he knew one thing for sure: the power of his personality. His innate leadership was confirmed by his role as a high school politician, and his determination was honed while he worked his way through college as a genial bartender and x-ray technician. If no one would hire him, he would start his own business, selling insurance. "I borrowed $1,000, sold my first policy, and hired a secretary." Within three years, Rick qualified for one of the insurance industry's most prestigious awards, "Top of the Table," for selling more than $100 million worth of policies in one year.

"From there, I started saving my money and buying other businesses. Over the next 40 years, I probably ended up buying and selling about 16 businesses." In 1993, for example, Rick sold an insurance and securities firm with $50 million in annual revenues. "I was 47 and able to work as a consultant while pursuing philanthropic projects." Not bad for a guy who never knew his father and whose single mother parked him for his first six years with her parents in rural Florida in a rickety row house heated only by the kitchen stove. Rick spent the next seven years living in trailer parks with his mother and her third husband until they moved to Mexico after dropping Rick off at a local boarding school. He was 13. "That left a cold place in my heart for my mother," Rick recalls.

Rick couldn't hold a job for the same reason he went to three different colleges and became a professional skydiver. He had ADD, which made it hard for him to focus, except when he was hurtling through space. "I worked for a company for a year and a half, and I did every corporate maneuver incorrectly," he recalls with the benefit of 40 years of hindsight and some effective psychotherapy. "The corporate environment would just get in the way—too many protocols and slow decisions."

Rick quickly decided to do exactly what many of the other successful entrepreneurs with disabilities I know have done: He created a custom-made environment (also known as a *startup*) that played to his strengths while minimizing his particular liabilities. Rick's modus operandi was to drink a pot of coffee by 9 a.m., which powered him through his to-do list. "But I would leave a wake of bodies along the way," he confesses. After selling his first company, Rick finally figured out, at age 42, how to ensure that his next company was better managed. "I found myself an 'accountability partner' to help me stay out of trouble." His wife, Janice, also knew how to rein him in. With experience and the right kind of people around him, Rick turned his intensity and breadth of interests into assets. His ADD gave him a competitive edge.

Rick is far from the only entrepreneur I know who had to learn how to turn a disadvantage into a strength. David Ash spent the first 30 years of his life in and out of so much trouble that it's amazing he didn't end up in jail. School was such a challenge that "by sixth grade I stopped trying."[2] He distinguished himself in the tough inner-city neighborhood of Montreal by "fighting, stealing, and skipping school." At 16, his main extracurricular activities were smoking weed and selling it. He also had epilepsy, which made life even more difficult.

David's parents were too occupied with their own challenges to monitor the behavior of their three sons. His father was an alcoholic railway dock loader living from paycheck to paycheck. His mentally ill mother was prone to prescription drug overdoses. David's first real job was washing pots at the YMCA. After that, he joined an apartment-hunting agency, which helped him find his inner salesman. At 17, he enrolled in a real estate course, which, to his amazement, he passed. "I finally had proof I wasn't fatally flawed." He was hired by a Century 21 agency and began wearing a fake mustache to look older. At a convention geared to inspire agents to set big goals, David vowed that he would be a millionaire by age 30. Over the next 10 years, he created one business after another, "some of which paid the bills."

At 30, David was living in Toronto, trying to recover from bankruptcy due to a $125,000 bill for six years of back taxes. To make another fresh start, he decided to move to Vancouver with his girlfriend Lise, a straight-arrow French Canadian nurse who saw something in David that he had yet to grasp. Within two years, they were married, working, saving money, and raising a baby boy. Blessed with the stable family he never had, David finally faced up to the omnipresent threat to that happiness: his drug habit. He joined Narcotics Anonymous.

When his daughter was born two years later, David, still clean, launched a new startup. With one employee and a small office, he became the second person to enter Canada's payday loan industry. Within a year, people were lining up outside the office for loans. Despite the controversy surrounding payday loans, David called it a "financial taxi" to help hardworking people with bad credit, strapped for cash, make it to their next payday.

Clearly, the company was filling a demand. Over the next three years, he opened 12 retail outlets across Canada. It was 1998, the dot-com boom was under way, and David seized the opportunity to grow even bigger by creating the first fully integrated online payday loan service. Four years later, that tiny company David had started had grown to 500 employees processing hundreds of millions of dollars in loans and generating millions in profits. David was the sole shareholder and richer than his younger self could ever have imagined.

So why was he still feeling that something was missing? The answer came in a class on how to use your business as a positive force, sponsored by the Entrepreneurs' Organization, a peer-to-peer group David had joined for professional and financial advice. A classmate explained how his company donated 20 percent of its profits to help the poor around the world and gave another 25 percent to his employees, plus two weeks of extra paid vacation if they promised to use it to help others.

David was stunned. "It's just how we were raised," his fellow entrepreneur explained. "I'm a Christian." Within a year, David had become a Christian and set up his own company fund donating $30,000 a month to organizations that provided food, shelter, and services to Vancouver's homeless and mentally ill. In 2004, he bought a derelict property in the city's poorest neighborhood and turned it into a refuge for 24 homeless women also suffering from mental health and addiction issues. He named it *The Vivian*, after his mother. Realizing that he cared more about his charitable work than his business, David decided to sell his company and become a social entrepreneur.

He and Lise bought a 71-room building in Vancouver, the Dodson, and restored it to provide transitional housing for local homeless people getting back on their feet. In 2014, David and Lise's foundation sold the Dodson—"at a considerable discount to market," notes David—to their operating partner, a community housing nonprofit that continues to run the facility.

One of the things I have learned from listening to all these successful entrepreneurs is to avoid measuring success only by the amount of wealth an individual has created. Much more interesting to me is the distance the person has traveled. I am almost always more fascinated by the amazing stories of successful entrepreneurs who have had to travel a longer distance to get to their success. Sometimes the starting point is moved back by disadvantaged parents; sometimes by the entrepreneur's addictions or learning disabilities, which have to be overcome or offset; and sometimes by some kind of unimaginable bad luck. The successful entrepreneurs who have the most to teach are often the ones who have had to overcome the most extreme adversities just to get to the starting line. They make the rest look easy.

Notes

1. Rick Gornto, interview (February 4, 2016).
2. David Ash, interview (October 24, 2016).

LESSON 8

Your Significant Other Must Enjoy Roller Coasters

I considered making this lesson number one, if only because the right partner—or certainly the wrong one—will inform every stage of your journey as an entrepreneur. In Tiger 21, as part of each member's annual Portfolio Defense, they are asked to share their list of the top 10 lessons they have learned so far. A common denominator is some version of the following exhortation: Marry the right person; it makes all the difference. "It wouldn't have happened," recalled one member who left a successful job to start a business with a very large personal loan, "if I hadn't married a woman willing to take a risk. I know so many people who won't let their husbands or wives take a risk to get ahead."

Linda and Magid Abraham are a particularly inspiring example of marriage working well. Linda and Magid met in 1985 through work. Linda was a marketing analyst at Procter & Gamble, and Magid, who had recently gotten a PhD from MIT, was working for a consulting company that Procter & Gamble had hired. As Linda puts it: "Ours is a relationship steeped in very geeky data."[1]

By 1992 they were married, and three years later they started Paragren, their first company together. It provided software for customer relationship management, and Linda and Magid sold it within two years. Then they moved on to their next venture, ComScore, which is where their entrepreneurial efforts paid off.

47

Partnership in love and business worked for the Abrahams from the start. "We are very complementary," says Linda. "He is very good at the strategic vision. And I am very good at commercializing. At knowing what the client needs. We are both very confident in what we're good at and what we're not good at."

More than two decades later, they are still working together. After working side by side for 14 years together on ComScore, they are now working on Upskill, a platform for wearable software like Google Glass. And they've managed to raise four kids along the way. "He's been my partner at every single step," says Linda.

"We have a very natural rhythm," Linda says of the way they've shared work and family responsibilities. "It's always been very fluid. A lot of women are faced with the choice of being all in or all out," she says of the decision to focus on children or continue to pursue an ambitious career. "I was in a very unique position to be able to do both."

Some people don't get it. "We get a lot of eyebrows raised at cocktail parties," says Linda. But for this pair of entrepreneurs, it just works. "Rather than being harder, it's made everything easier. I don't know if I could have accomplished what I have without him. Our interests are always 100 percent aligned," she says. "I don't buy into the whole work/life balance thing. For me it's just life."

The Abrahams' model is exceptional. Not many people find romantic and professional partnership in the same person. Most entrepreneurs I know have had a significant other who was willing to play a supporting role.

Robert Oringer's wife, Marla, actually encouraged him to quit his very good job at IBM and go into business for himself. They were engaged to be married at the time, and Marla, who had started dating Robert when she was a teenager, had just finished her business degree and was planning to get a job in retail fashion. "I never envisioned myself being married to a company guy—all I knew were family businesses," explains Marla, whose father owned a successful garment business in Montreal.[2] "Don't you want to leave to do something else?" she asked Robert, well aware that starting his own business had been his goal since he'd switched his major at the Wharton School from accounting to entrepreneurial management. Robert said that he had planned to stay at IBM for five years. "Well, you're approaching five," Marla noted. "Don't you think it's enough?" Robert thought about it for a moment and then said, "Yeah, I think you're right."[3]

Robert began looking for a business to buy in New York or Montreal, and with the help of business brokers Marla's father introduced him to, an opportunity turned up in Montreal. "Three weeks before the wedding,"

Marla recalls, "Robert called and said, 'I'm moving up to Montreal.'" A few days before the wedding, they bought the business with wedding gifts and a $70,000 loan from Marla's father. "We got married, there was no honeymoon, just a couple of nights in a hotel in Montreal. And at the end of the weekend, Robert left for Vancouver on his first business trip. That was okay with me because I knew we were setting ourselves up. It was part of the whole process for me." Marla was 22, married to an inexperienced entrepreneur with a struggling company and a loan. Robert remembers his state of mind at the time: He would wake up at night "scared to death."

Marla didn't know that, but Robert did share with her his plans for developing the business. In the meantime, Marla had quickly found and furnished an apartment for them and landed a job as a fashion buyer, which she liked. "I was pursuing my own career because it was my income that was supporting us," she explained. She wanted a family but made it clear that she was willing to wait several years to start it in order to give her husband a chance to grow the business. "We lived modestly," she says. "I wasn't complaining. Our conversation was about building our life together. I saw my role as being supportive in any way, shape, or form to get us out of the gate."

Above all, Marla saw herself as "a partner." That partnership got much stronger—and more complicated—eight years later. By then, Robert was tasting some success as an entrepreneur, having merged his company with another company where he had developed a partnership with the two owners of the company his merged with.

After five good years as a buyer, Marla had quit to take over leadership of a division of her father's company after the unexpected death of her uncle, who had been president of the division. "I was now selling to retailers, and the buyers liked me because they knew I had been a retailer too," she recalls. She continued traveling for the company well into the eighth month of her first pregnancy, taking only a few months off after their first son, Cory, was born. When their second son, Justin, was born, Marla went back to work after just a few weeks.

When Justin was nine months old and Cory was three, both boys were diagnosed with diabetes within three weeks of each other. Marla was doing blood sugar tests throughout the nights, going to work exhausted, and still traveling one to two days a week. "It was not going well," she confesses. "I knew I had to make some changes. So I turned off the lights in my office and told my dad and everybody in my division that I'd be back in a month." But she never returned. "After a couple of days at home, as sad as I was not working, I was hit with the double reality that managing two young children with diabetes was a 24/7 endeavor, and that I needed to support Robert so that he could do what he needed to do to be successful. Our lives had changed." As an entrepreneur selling diabetes-related products, Robert was well versed in what families were up against long before his children were diagnosed. His path now became very clear to him. It was, in his words, "To develop products to improve the lives of my children."

While Robert refocused on breakthrough products and investments related to diabetes, Marla sat outside her kids' nursery, pre-K, kindergarten, and elementary school classrooms, checking their sugar levels every half hour and advising their teachers on care. When the Oringers could afford household help, she trained and supervised them. "That was my job, seven days a week, my own little company of around-the-clock help," she recalls. "And we discussed everything that Robert was doing in his business related to diabetes, so we were really partners."

Marla's advice to young couples starting out their lives with a partner who is trying to launch a business: "Somebody has to be grounded in that relationship in order to allow that entrepreneur to thrive. So at the beginning of our careers, I was the grounded one who had the stable job in Montreal. I was not making waves. I was there to be leaned upon. I was the support." Marla clearly held up her side of the partnership: Cory is now working at Goldman Sachs in New York. Justin is at the University of Southern California pursuing his passion for the business side of music. And with the nest now empty, Marla has entered a new stage of her partnership with Robert. "I was always a partner in his investments," she explains. "But now I'm traveling with him, going to meetings with the founders of diabetes-focused start-ups, socializing with other potential co-investors, and being introduced as 'partner.' Up to now I've always been his support, but now he's helping me find my new passion."

Robert has helped Marla take her work with diabetes-related projects to a global scale. In the fall of 2015, she joined the Leadership Council of Beyond Type 1, a new California-based nonprofit creating programs and innovations to help people with diabetes around the world thrive. "The goal is also to change the conversation about diabetes and make people aware of what people living with diabetes have to deal with day to day," explains Marla, who will be buying and sourcing all of Beyond Type 1's branded merchandise. In September 2015, she also began advising on the public relations and social media efforts for *The Human Trial*, a documentary film following the efforts of a company that is searching for a cure for diabetes.

Rick Gornto (Lesson 7) and his wife, Janice, began their entrepreneurial journey a generation before the Oringers; they have been married for 45 years. When they met, Rick was 25 and had just taken some time off from his first semester of law school to recover from breaking his neck skydiving. While recovering, he met a devout Christian who was such a good guy that Rick decided he wanted to be just like him. Rick became a churchgoer—and then his mentor introduced him to his niece. "I like to say," Rick says, "that at age 25, I met *the two* Js—Jesus and Janice, who have been very good for me."[4]

"We started from scratch," he recalls. "I mean, we had nothing." But Rick's belief in himself, and Janice's faith that he would succeed, amazingly, turned out to be all they needed. "I was so naïve and trusting," recalls Janice, laughing at her twenty-something self, just out of college with a degree in speech therapy, newly married, and soon to be a mother. "It didn't start out so well," she confesses.[5] At first, Rick had trouble finding and keeping a job. Then he grabbed an opportunity with an insurance company in a suburb of Houston, moving there while Janice was pregnant with their second child. "It was kind of crazy," she admits, noting that Rick was not getting a regular salary: "It was commission only."

But Rick quickly proved to be a natural salesman, the commissions increased, and so did his confidence in his business abilities. "Rick was such a go-getter and self-motivator," marvels Janice, conceding that by nature she was way more cautious and analytical, just the kind of person Rick needed to balance out his attention deficit disorder and impulsive nature. With Janice as his anchor—"I'm always keeping him on track," she says— Rick's reputation as a talented insurance salesman spread. He soon became a partner in another insurance company in town and began saving for his next move. Janice considered returning to school to become a nurse but quickly realized that Rick's work was becoming too unpredictable for her to take a regular job. "Someone like Rick, eager to run his own businesses, needs a partner who can turn on a dime," she explains. "He might call me from work on a Monday and say, 'We're going to Hawaii on Friday. There's this meeting; we've got to be there.' I had to immediately find a sitter to take care of the kids and get going. If I had a career, I wouldn't have been able to do things like that."

In retrospect, Janice has trouble believing how trusting she was. "If my daughter came to me and said, 'My husband wants to quit his job and take a commission-only job, and I'm pregnant, and we're moving,'" I'd be saying, "'Are you crazy?'" Then she laughs: "And so the moral of that story is that sometimes you just have to be young and stupid."

Or very, very optimistic, which, as I've noted, is an essential trait of the successful entrepreneur. (And let me quickly add that not all the entrepreneurs I know have had marriages as successful as the Abrahams, Gorntos, and Oringers.) For Janice, sharing a life with an entrepreneur requires one trait above all: "You have to be flexible." She has no regrets and would recommend the entrepreneur's life to anyone who sought her advice: "You will have an exciting life," she says. "You'll meet lots of people, go to lots of places, and life will never be dull for you." Amen to that.

As I tried to frame the takeaway here, I was reminded that my own good fortune is similar to Rick's and Robert's, in that my wife of 40 years has also gone along with an ever-changing entrepreneurial life. Katja came from an extremely successful real estate family. If I had lost everything along the way, our kids would never have starved. This allowed me to take risks I might otherwise have thought long and hard about. Like Marla Oringer, Katja also understood the life of the entrepreneur in a fundamental way, having grown up with a father who was his own boss and suffered some significant ups and downs along the way.

When I had to drop everything for a deal or something related to a business I owned, my wife has been, in a thousand ways, more flexible and tolerant than most other wives would be, for which I am forever grateful. (Family emergencies still come first, and so do major life events, most of the time.)

For Rick, Robert, and me, the model was pretty conventional. Our wives played critical support roles, often doing most of the day-to-day work of raising a family and running a home. That career isn't paid, but it can be just as taxing as running any business. Yet this is only one way of doing things—there are clearly other ways to make family, marriage, and entrepreneurship work. Linda and Magid are an important example of a different type of partnership.

I'll close with this warning: Once you've committed to the entrepreneur's journey, you should think twice about forming a lifelong relationship with someone who isn't prepared to be supportive or, worse still, whose emotional or personal needs will prevent you from having the flexibility and capacity required to weather the inevitable storms that will arise throughout your career. If you possibly can, choose someone who is prepared to be your partner in every way.

Notes

1. Linda Abraham, interview (February 3, 2017).
2. Marla Oringer, interview (August 11, 2016).
3. Robert Oringer, interview (July 21, 2016).
4. Rick Gornto, interview (February 4, 2016).
5. Janice Gornto, interview (August 15, 2016).

STAGE 2

Team Building

The archetype of the great American entrepreneur is the solitary genius who singlehandedly turns an idea that everyone else thought was crazy into an iconic company. But when you get a group of entrepreneurs together in a room, you'll quickly find out that most of them reaped the benefit of the talents and strengths of others—trusted advisors, partners, managers, and employees—at every step along the way.

You're Never Too Smart—or Too Old—for a Mentor

Line up any group of people from least to most successful, and you are likely to find that the ones in the more successful half of the line have had deep experiences with mentors. That's especially the case with entrepreneurs. The other half of the line will have lots of excuses why they never were able to find the right person to be their mentor. "It saves a lot of time, frustration, and mistakes if you have someone who knows what he's doing giving you advice," says John Bridge from Chicago, who has depended on mentors while starting four different businesses.

I have benefited from multiple mentors, beginning with the president of the company I worked for in my first full-time job at 17, through every stage of my career. Mentors have helped me become a better entrepreneur, investor, manager, citizen, and, I like to think, person. By definition, a mentor is an experienced guide. The term derives from the character Mentor in the *Odyssey*, whom Odysseus put in charge of his household and only son Telemachus before he set off for the Trojan War.

Mentors can play any number of roles, depending on your needs:

- **Wise veteran**—Willing to give a younger person the benefit of her experience and success.
- **Eager teacher**—Willing to pass on specific knowledge and skills to newcomers, peers, or, in the case of new technologies, superiors.
- **Generous peer**—Willing to help colleagues or friends learn skills, gain information, network new business contacts, and avoid mistakes the mentor has made in the past.
- **Life coach**—Willing (or trained) to advise others about personal goals, career opportunities, and family issues related to a career, business, and retirement.
- **Good listener**—Sometimes the most important thing a person dealing with challenging issues needs is a trusted mentor to listen to them explain the issues and explore solutions. The simple act of discussing your deepest concerns or quandaries with someone you trust often allows you to explore options and solutions that might never have emerged in solitude. There is a reason why psychoanalysis is so powerful even when so much of the time the patient is talking and the analyst is *merely* listening.

When I was cooking up my first real estate development venture in the early 1980s, all I knew was that I needed help. Desperately.

I had finished college and had a few years of work under my belt, but I had never developed anything in my life, let alone a building that had been the largest building in the world when it was built in 1929 (the Pentagon unseated it in 1943). The building was the Harborside Terminal, the intermodal freight and warehousing facility built by the Pennsylvania Railroad as its northeastern United States distribution center, which could serve 4 ships, 78 railcars, and 128 trucks simultaneously, sometimes around the clock. When I was first introduced to Harborside, it was right out of Marlon Brando's famous movie *On the Waterfront*, which took place about a mile north along the Hudson River in Hoboken, the northern neighbor to Jersey City, New Jersey.

Among the skeptics was my father-in-law, who co-owned the property at the time with his brother. They were very major owner-operators of a real estate empire that controlled properties all over the New York metropolitan area. While Harborside was a monster of a building in its own right, it was just one of many industrial buildings they owned. Harborside was both a landlord to many different types of industrial tenants and a warehousing company in its own right, which stored all sorts of things—industrial goods like printing presses, consumer goods ranging from motorcycles to calculators, and such commodities as coffee, spices, and cocoa beans. My father-in-law and his brother had a strategy to let tired industrial buildings in tough neighborhoods pay for themselves as working warehouses until the neighborhood changed—sometimes decades later. They knew how to hold on to properties for the long term, but they were not developers. They let the developers buy their appreciated properties at prices that dwarfed what they had paid for them.

When they looked at my vision for Harborside, all they could see was the downside of getting into the development-construction business, which would require a more complex organization in which extremely important decisions would have to be delegated to employees (perhaps to me). That wasn't their style, and it represented risks they were uncomfortable with.

I was eager to prove them and all the other skeptics wrong. And, as I like to joke, it was the last time I could really afford to lose everything I had.

How to proceed, however, was a mystery. I had taken the idea as far as I could. I needed a partner who could attract the level of financing necessary to acquire the terminal and begin developing it. But how does a 24-year-old find such a partner? I had no idea.

Then I got lucky. My wife and I were having our first business dinner (ever) with a real estate guru who had been a consultant on a project in California that I had worked on at Goldman Sachs. I had called him in California and told him about my idea, and as luck would have it, he was coming to New York. The next day after our dinner, he happened to be meeting with an old friend of his, David Fromer, who had just returned to the U.S. with his family after a decade working abroad. The consultant told David about "a kid with a big idea you should pursue." Two days later, David walked into my office, and I gave him my pitch—the complete presentation that I had slaved over for a year. The issue that concerned everyone else about my project—how big it was—seemed to excite David. After discussing the details for a couple of hours, he said, "Let's do it." And just like that, I had a partner.

We were definitely an odd couple. I had spent a year at Goldman Sachs, only part of it in the real estate department. David had spent 30 years developing real estate in Los Angeles, London, and Saudi Arabia. The Vietnam War had ended while I was still in high school; David had seen plenty of action in Europe in World War II, winning three Purple Hearts and a Bronze Star for bravery in combat.

But I was thrilled. Here was this guy who had worked on real estate all over the world, and he bought my vision. We went to work, experiencing many downs as well as ups. After 18 months and a couple of false starts, we finally put together the $25 million in financing needed to acquire the Harborside Terminal (as 50–50 partners), which quickly became America's largest commercial renovation project.

Today, looking west from downtown Manhattan across the Hudson River, you see endless high-rises sprouting up virtually everywhere, but when we started Harborside's transformation in 1982 there wasn't a single commercial high-rise under construction on the Jersey side of the Hudson River for as far as the eye could see.

When we sold the Harborside Financial Center, having completed the first million square feet of conversions, the Governor's Waterfront Development Office told the *New York Times* that our project "helped to spur interest in all waterfront development"[1] on the Hudson River coastline stretching from Jersey City north, past the George Washington Bridge in Fort Lee.

Thanks to David's qualities as a mentor, I learned much about real estate development, wheeling and dealing in New Jersey politics, and life in general that I might have never figured out over an entire career.

David had a pithy way of framing his insights. For example: *There is no such thing as good and bad real estate, just good and bad deals.* No matter how objectively terrible a piece of real estate may be, if you can buy it cheaply enough, it can still be a very good deal. Conversely (and perhaps far more important), no matter how impressive a piece of real estate might be, if you pay too much for it, you reduce your safety margin, perhaps to the point of ensuring a bad deal. Simple strategies like not overpaying are, in my experience, much underappreciated.

After we sold Harborside, David and I pursued our own independent businesses, but we often invested in each other's business activities. For the next 25 years, until he died in 2010 at age 86, David remained my best friend, a father figure (even though I had a father), a brother figure (even though I had a brother), and my most significant mentor. Most important of all, he was a great guy with the kind of humility and empathy that is too often missing among the business class. Every time I called David with a problem I was confronting he would say, "How can I help?" Knowing he was on my side was endlessly comforting.

As I recall David's wise advice and my long and productive relationship with him, another definition for mentor occurs to me: *Someone whose favorite words of wisdom echo in your head long after he is gone.* I am still quoting one insight or another that David drilled into me over those 30 years. My experience with David and a number of other mentors I've had has convinced me that having a veteran advisor in your corner in your first job (and subsequent gigs too) is even more important to the success of your career than a big salary or title. The money will be spent and long forgotten, but your mentor's words, if you are lucky, will echo in your head for a lifetime.

How do you find a mentor? There are endless ways, but just as a journey of a thousand miles starts with a single step, the first step toward finding a mentor is to be on the lookout for one. As the famous parable suggests: When the student is ready, the teacher will arrive.

Note

1. "Jersey Waterfront Project Sold for $120 Million," *New York Times* (November 28, 1986).

Mentors Are Available for the Price of Asking

I've asked a number of entrepreneurs who have benefited from mentors about how they found them, and most did it the old-school way—they asked. "There's a lot of nice people out there who want to mentor others, many of them because they had also benefited from mentors. All you have to do is ask them," advises John Bridge, an entrepreneur based in Chicago.[1]

It also helps if you display the ambition and energy the young John Bridge did. After a stint in the U.S. Air Force, John enrolled in a local college to study business. While his classmates were competing for top grades as their ticket to job security, John had already learned that no such thing exists. His father had worked for 28 years for the same company until the day the owner decided to sell the business. "My father ended up without a job and with five kids."

John viewed college as an opportunity to find an area where he could get into business for himself as quickly as possible. One day, a guest lecturer turned up in his real estate class to talk about property tax liens, something that John knew nothing about. The lecturer, a local real estate entrepreneur named Barrett Rochman, explained to the class that municipalities and counties depend on property taxes to bankroll public services and government employees. When a home or business owner doesn't pay those taxes, eventually the county obtains a lien against the property. If the taxes remain unpaid for a certain period of time, the lien can be auctioned off to private investors willing to pay the taxes immediately to allow the government to have the resources to operate. Investors buy the liens—known as *tax certificates*—at public auctions by bidding down the rate of interest that the delinquent owner will be charged as a penalty for nonpayment. The lowest bidder wins the certificate, which generally might yield as much as 8 to 10 percent. By all accounts, tax certificates are pretty safe investments, because most taxpayers are inclined to pay off the lien before the penalties add up or they lose their property to foreclosure, which is what happens if the tax liens are not eventually paid off.

Intrigued, John did some calculations on a piece of paper, and after class he approached the lecturer with a proposition. "This looks like a great business. If I'm interested in doing Northern Illinois, would you partner with me?" Impressed by the student's chutzpah, Rochman warned John that he would have to get very serious about the tax business, studying local laws and procedures as well as the fine points of the real estate business to make sure the properties he was investing in were valuable enough to sell for a profit. Rochman also hit the kid with an even bigger dose of reality: to become a major player in Northern Illinois would require raising about $70 million in capital. John didn't flinch. "Being a dumb college kid, I figured I could raise the money quickly."

That didn't happen, of course. But after graduation, lacking any acceptable job offers, John asked Rochman to take him under his wing. John spent the next two years learning as much as he could about the intricacies of Illinois real estate, tax liens, and sheriffs' sale businesses while attending local tax sales looking for deals.

At one of the sales, John began talking to an older man in his early sixties who confided that he had invested $150,000 in a local lien company, which didn't seem to know what it was doing. John became friendly with that man, Joe Somario, and eventually offered to handle those tax certificates and get Somario's money back, which he did. "I never charged him a dime," says John, who assumed that his new friend was just another small investor. Somario turned out to be a successful entrepreneur worth millions—and he became John's second mentor.

Over the next five years, John worked seven days a week with his mentors to build a tax business, including a new design for organizing the data, as he was also learning how to raise the necessary capital. "Yes, I was starting at square one, but I had the benefit of 20 years of experience as a result of having these two mentors behind me who were saying, 'Maybe you shouldn't do that,' or 'Do this,'" John recalls. "They saved me from wasting a lot of time on mistakes." John was soon mentoring his less computer-literate mentors on the advantages of building an updatable computerized database of the property tax records around the state, which allowed them to better predict the rate of return on delinquent properties and thus underbid their competitors.

The only thing that they lacked to reach their goal to be the biggest players in the property tax business in Northern Illinois was capital. Then, in 1993, Somario called John about an article he had read "about this guy in Florida who has the opposite problem you have," meaning he had plenty of capital and was looking for opportunities. His name was Richard Heitmeyer, and he was a 54-year-old entrepreneur who, according to the article, had persuaded Lehman Brothers, the Wall Street investment bank, that he could build a multibillion-dollar business out of buying tax liens. He only needed the capital to establish himself as a nationwide player in a market dominated by local operators. Lehman reportedly had committed one billion dollars.

Somario bought his young protégé a plane ticket to Florida, where John delivered a presentation to Heitmeyer on the property tax business in Illinois. "Two hours later I walked out of there with a handshake agreement that I could do Illinois, with access to $100 million. I know that sounds far-fetched, but it's the honest-to-God truth," John recalls, laughing at the memory.

A year later, John and Somario were on the front page of the *Chicago Sun Times* for having bought the largest single tax certificate in the United States for $7.2 million. It was John's 30th birthday. By bringing Wall Street money to the auctions, John had helped revolutionize the U.S. tax lien business. Not bad for a guy whose high school guidance counselor told him that he would never be fit for more than a blue-collar job.

John is now a successful entrepreneur with one hand still in the tax lien business and the other launching two new businesses making technological and marketing breakthroughs in radio broadcasting. A risky move for a property tax specialist whose only previous experience with radio was listening to it in the car? Not if you have the right mentor. John's new mentor is an entrepreneur who has bought, owned, and sold hundreds of radio stations. "I'm learning more about terrestrial radio broadcasting than I ever wanted to know," he says, laughing. In his free time, John is also mentoring his college-age sons in the art of profiting from property tax certificates and real estate.

Note

1. John Bridge, interview (July 8, 2015).

The Right Partner Can Multiply Your Potential

I was lucky to find a partner who not only helped me achieve my vision, but was also a mentor who taught me lessons that I continue to benefit from. Many of the successful entrepreneurs I know turned the concept of a partnership into a strategic tool throughout their careers—both for maximizing their own personal potential to succeed and for driving their business models.

I've known Ron Bruder for more than a decade. My admiration for how he has managed his phenomenally successful career has only grown over the years. Ask him about his success, and the first thing he'll talk about is the value of partnerships.

First, a bit about Ron. Ron grew up in a hardworking family in a rough neighborhood of Brooklyn. "My parents gave me the belief that I could achieve whatever I wanted," he recalls.[1] At 17, he was selling encyclopedias. He created a profitable business by hiring stay-at-home mothers to make phone solicitations and paying their kids to slip proposals through doors. After studying physics and then economics in college on scholarship, he also went on to earn an MBA. Then Ron took over a distressed travel agency in Clifton, New Jersey. Within a few months, he talked his way onto the American Airlines Sabre computer network, increasing his traffic exponentially. It is hard to appreciate how ahead of his time Ron was. Sabre was the first computerized airline reservation system. The mid-1970s were still

20 years away from a functioning Internet. In fact, the entire Sabre reservation system existed in a single computer center, which travel agents called into until the mid-70s. Then, in 1976, Sabre installed online terminals in the first 130 travel agencies. It took extraordinary foresight and Ron's salesmanship to get his travel agency to be one of the first travel agencies in the country to have this advanced tool that would revolutionize the entire travel industry. Ron was in the vanguard, and he created huge upside value in his travel agency.

He sold the agency and, in 1977, founded the Brookhill Group (named for his uphill climb out of Brooklyn), a real estate company that specialized in developing and turning around shopping centers as well as industrial and office buildings. In the 1990s, Brookhill created a special niche as the nation's premier redeveloper of brownfields, environmentally polluted land that must be cleaned up as part of the redevelopment process. The company has operated real estate in 22 states, with a total value of more than three-quarters of a billion dollars.

On top of that, Ron also founded a medical technology company and an oil and gas business. And since 2006, he has worked full-time establishing Education for Employment (EFE), an international foundation to create employment opportunities for young men and women in the Middle East and North Africa (www.efe.org).

What was the common denominator that helped him climb that hill out of Brooklyn and into an extraordinarily varied and productive career as a serial entrepreneur and philanthropist? "Good partnerships," says Ron. "I've been in good deals with bad partners and bad deals with good partners. I would definitely choose the latter."

The approach he adopted at Brookhill epitomizes Ron's use of partnerships to achieve more than might have been possible on his own. Unlike most other investors who walked away from the potential liabilities of properties burdened by both real and perceived environmental contamination, Ron came up with an ingenious strategy that would help him turn such distressed assets into gold. First, he partnered with a world-class environmental engineering firm, Dames & Moore, that provided him with the capability to clean up pollutants on brownfield sites. Then, he found a large insurance company that would underwrite a new product called *environmental insurance*, which insured buyers of previously contaminated properties against any remaining pollution. Finally, he partnered with Credit Suisse, which securitized the debt so that the risk could be spread out among investors who provided the necessary capital to restore the land and buildings.

In his 30-plus-year career, Ron has been burned by sketchy partners. "One guy stole three and a half million dollars," he told me. He has identified three qualities to look for in a good partner:

1. They do what they say they will.
2. They have a track record of doing what they say they will.
3. They have shared values and similar visions of where the partnership may lead.

To achieve his foundation's goals in the Middle East, Ron notes, "We spend a lot of time figuring out whom to partner with, doing really careful diligence."

Entrepreneur Jeff Scheck also believes in the importance of partnerships, but instead of looking for partners, his family company set out to create them. In 1956, Jeff's grandfather, Samuel, had bought a paper mill in Syracuse, New York, and moved it to Cuba. Three years later, he found himself with a partner who certainly didn't share his values or vision. "In 1959, Castro became our 100 percent partner when he nationalized my family's paper mill in Cuba," Jeff explains. "We fled to Miami."[2]

Burdened with more than $500,000 in debt that he had borrowed from Georgia Pacific to build the business in Cuba, Jeff's grandfather came up with a plan. As Jeff tells it, his grandfather "asked Georgia Pacific for some materials and products so that he could begin distributing them and create a business that would generate adequate cash for repayment." That was the origin of Sweet Paper Sales, which over the next 50 years became one of America's largest wholesale distributors of paper, food services, and commercial janitorial and sanitation products. Jeff's grandfather eventually handed the reins to Jeff's father, Michael. Jeff and his siblings were innovative vice presidents who kept the business growing. Their clients included hotels, offices, and especially restaurants, which turned out to be why the Schecks sold Sweet Paper in 2005 to a major janitorial/sanitation paper company that wanted to increase its footprint in food services. With 450 employees, 10 distribution centers around the country, and $250 million in sales, it had the resources to acquire Sweet Paper.

At the root of Sweet Paper's success, according to Jeff, was a philosophy that focused on nurturing a partnership spirit among all parties. "We always treated vendors, customers, and employees like family. When we made mistakes, we fixed them. When we made promises, we fulfilled them." Jeff and his brother Marty talked their father into incentivizing managers with a share of any profits they generated. "He thought we were crazy. He green-lighted the idea skeptically. But his skepticism vanished when one of those highly incentivized managers increased his sales by a million dollars in a single year," Jeff recalls with a laugh, noting that those tuition payments his father paid for Jeff to attend the University of Pennsylvania's Wharton School and for Marty to get degrees at Columbia and the University of Miami's business school were maybe worth it after all. "We worked hard to find the right employees and we were happy to share profits with them—creating businesses within businesses to empower people into being more entrepreneurial."

For Jeff, this successful partnership strategy was simply an offshoot of the principle at the center of the Schecks' family values. "We treated others as we wanted to be treated." Sounds to me like one more key to finding and keeping a good partner.

Notes

1. Ron Bruder, interview (December 2012).
2. Jeff Scheck, interview (September 3, 2015).

Know When to Be Nice

We've all been in a position where we feel we have to choose between being nice and being tough. You're probably thinking, "I'm struggling to keep this business alive. Not everyone is pulling their weight. I'm going to have to fire people. And you expect me to be nice?!"

Please know that I spent 25 years trying to drag one of my companies into the black. Personally, I'd lost millions of dollars, and the frustration and resentment I felt in the face of the employees' long line of failures were driving me to such distraction that, frankly, I was not all that nice. I was beginning to feel that I cared about many of our employees' jobs more than they did. In retrospect, my irritation was probably, in part, a reflection of my own limitations as a manager.

Most entrepreneurs I know came up in a highly competitive business culture driven by a "nice guys finish last" philosophy. Successful companies, particularly private ones, are not democracies; founders and CEOs are the last of the dictators. The media, whether on reality TV shows like *The Apprentice* or on the business news networks, endlessly promote the view that you have to be tough and even ruthless to dominate your market. But almost all the best entrepreneurs I know have learned a very different lesson from their careers: to put a premium on what today's management gurus call *social skills*. "I learned firsthand that if your employees are happy, it's amazing how far they will go on your behalf," says Pete Settle.[1]

In 1999, Pete founded a school bus company with his three brothers as his management team. They had some experience in the field. The Settles had had a transport business before, and they sold it to a large public corporation.

Pete had stayed on for six years afterward, rising to senior vice president of marketing and sales for the school bus division—until he realized that his 190 days a year on the road had turned him into a stranger to his own kids.

Pete's vision for the new bus company was audacious. He wanted to create an upside-down organization where his managers would serve the needs of their bus drivers and attendants. "Driving a school bus is a hard job," he explains, noting that drivers have to get up early to sit in a cold bus, show up twice a day, and deal with insolent kids. "We decided to make the bus lot a fun place to work."

That decision gave them an edge on the competition. They gave their drivers company shirts and jackets. They outfitted trailers with mobile grills that would show up on the bus lot to cook lunch for the drivers and attendants, and on hot days ice cream trucks would appear. The company spent 30 times what other companies budgeted for employee perks. "We could afford it," he says, "because we had many fewer accident claims and didn't have to pay as much workers' compensation as our competitors. We created an atmosphere where our people valued something about their employment with us. And when you have something to lose, you protect it—and maybe look in the mirror twice before making a right-hand turn or hitting a parked car." Pete also noted that a disgruntled employee who twisted an ankle getting into a bus on an icy day was inclined to file a compensation claim, but "if they're happy in the job, they often just walk it off."

The result was not just the happy bus lot that Pete had envisioned, but also a growing list of happy customers. Within three years, the company had several large contracts for county disability services and school districts, including the Cincinnati Public Schools. By 2012, Pete's company had 4,000 buses, 4,167 employees, 72 locations across 10 states, and sales of over $180 million. Those kinds of numbers caught the eye of an international transport company eager to expand its North America operations.

When to be nice is a lesson that the biggest corporations are just beginning to learn. In 2011, when Google decided to survey employees on the traits they valued in a manager, the assumption was that the top-ranking trait would be deep technical expertise. Google's leaders were stunned to learn that what employees wanted most were bosses available for one-on-one meetings, willing to help them work through problems and to take an interest in their lives.

Google employees valued bosses who were, in a word, *nice.* According to a 2015 study, most of the wage growth in the United States since 1980 has taken place in areas that require high cognitive and social skills that computers and robots cannot replicate. "The days of being able to plug away in isolation on a quantitative problem and be paid well for it are increasingly over," says David Deming, an economics professor at the Harvard Graduate School of Education.[2] Companies are looking for people who are not only book smart but also have emotional intelligence and are persuasive enough to negotiate and coordinate with colleagues.

The same thing that motivated Pete Settle's blue-collar bus drivers is exactly what had the biggest positive effect on Google's highly curated work-force: sympathetic managers. "Our best managers," reported Google's chief of human resources, "have teams that perform better, are retained better, are happier—they do everything better."[3] For Google, *best* turned out to be *nice*.

Pete has brought his experience as a manager to his new career in private equity, placing employee loyalty to the company leadership high on his checklist. "Recently, I wanted to buy the company of a friend of mine who engenders amazing loyalty in the people who work for him. There is nothing that will blow that unit apart." Unfortunately for Pete (and fortunately for his friend), the line of eager investors was too long and rich.

Keep this lesson in mind the next time you're wondering what's going wrong in your shop or what it will take to get the best out of your best people: Take a deep breath and be nice. It is an important start to enhancing your teams' performance.

Notes

1. Pete Settle, interview (June 15, 2015).
2. Nicole Torres, "Research: Technology Is Only Making Social Skills More Important," *Harvard Business Review* (August 26, 2015).
3. Adam Bryant, "Google's Quest to Build a Better Boss," *New York Times* (March 12, 2011).

LESSON 13

Hire for the Good—the Bad Comes at No Extra Expense

My partner David Fromer and I built a staff of almost 100 people to transform the Harborside Terminal into the Harborside Financial Center, while thousands of people continued working for our tenants in the facility on a daily basis. Undertaking a major construction project with people working all around you adds immense complexity and risk, but we had no choice. Today I am willing to concede that managing people is not my greatest strength. Back then I thought I knew what I was doing—or at least how a good manager should operate. After all, I had a master's degree in management.

Fortunately, I started out with someone who really did know what he was doing (or at least he knew a lot more than me). When David witnessed my frustration with one employee or another who just wasn't delivering, he offered one of his pithy sayings: "You hire for the good. The bad comes at no extra expense."

As any manager knows, when you're upset about something, it's hard to think about anything else. But David repeated that catchphrase enough times that when an employee's performance angered me, I was increasingly able to step back from my emotions and ask myself, "What is it that's good about this person? Why did we make the hire?" Focusing on the value that particular person was adding to our business helped me put what I didn't like into perspective.

Perhaps I was expecting the employee to achieve something that was beyond her expertise; maybe she didn't have the personality for a given task. Some people, for example, excel in meetings or making presentations; others do their best work holed up alone in their offices. If you've hired someone for his talent in sales, you should not be surprised that he's procrastinating on writing his section of the annual report. Similarly, that team manager who always seems so calm probably has stronger feelings than he reveals.

Sometimes you can give even your most talented employees more responsibility than they're ready for. What young managers don't realize is that the employee who can do it all is a rare bird. Many of the successful entrepreneurs I know learned this lesson by looking in the mirror. It took me years to concede that although my managerial skills improved with experience, they were not my strong suit. It took Pete Settle most of his career to realize that he was "an outside guy," good at dealing with clients and growing the business but unhappy when stuck behind a desk handling administrative tasks. "We all have our weakness," he observes. "I need to adapt my style to yours if I'm going to get out of you what I need."[1]

Raising those kinds of questions is an effective way of bringing down the boil of frustration and reducing the anxiety of employee relations. If there was more on the good side of the ledger than on the bad, I made accommodations. If there was not enough on the good side to balance the bad, I could justify replacing that employee or transferring them to a job they were better suited for. More important, if the employee's actions or behavior was putting the enterprise at risk in some material manner, I had no choice but to make a change. You must *always* do what is right for the organization first, and then once a decision is made, do what is right for the employee. Not the other way around. If terminating someone becomes necessary, this can be done by way of severance or other measures to help the person through the transition period.

Too many times I have seen organizations get caught up in a sticky staff decision and lose the courage to do what is right. Sometimes an employee continues to fail, and the careers of an entire team—the poor performer's colleagues—are unnecessarily harmed. Sometimes the entire organization ends up paying the price for a weak employee in some small or even big way.

Pete has benefited from the Insight Discovery system, which helps managers and employees get a better fix on their personality strengths and weaknesses so that they can develop better teamwork strategies. Using the celebrated psychologist Carl Jung's model of psychological types, it asks 50 questions designed to reveal four dominant personality traits, which are color coded: fiery red (high-energy extroverts, direct, authoritative), earth green (value-oriented, eager to be relied upon), sunshine yellow (radiant, friendly, positive), and cool blue (introverts, analytical, precise). The result is a 20-page personality profile identifying the respondent's unique strengths and weaknesses, style of communication, and how a person with those traits might bring value to a team.

This has helped Pete reap dividends from employees in ways that might never have occurred to him. For example, Pete himself scored fiery red, which didn't surprise him because his communication style has always been "keep it short and get to the point." Clued in to the reality of how different personality types operate, a manager can build a team whose members complement each other's strengths and weakness. Pete began entering a meeting ready to accommodate the comfort levels of the other people in the room. "The green person would like me to ask about how his daughter is doing in high school before we get going," he explains. "The blues—the analytical types—were a real challenge, and we used to joke about it."

Another commonly used tool is the Myers-Briggs test, also based on the work of Jung, and there are many others that evaluate personality, intelligence, and compatibility. But even without adopting a formal system of personality analysis, recognizing that we all have our different personality types, strengths, and weaknesses will make you a better manager. Putting high-performing teams together successfully requires assessing how individual team members will interact with one another. Understanding what combinations of people (or personality traits) will enhance or diminish a team's ability to work together effectively can give a leader a leg up.

Common insights among the most experienced and successful leaders I know are variations of the following: "You have to empower your people and your teams." That's a lot easier to do if you work to figure out what individual team members' strengths are—the good that you hired them for in the first place—and build teams that allow each person's particular skills to shine because the mix of the team has been devised to give the greatest chance of the most effective collective action.

Note

1. Pete Settle, interview (June 30, 2015).

LESSON 14

Surround Yourself with People Who Are Smarter Than You

Most of the successful entrepreneurs I have known—including the guy I look at in the mirror—have a tendency to overrate their personal skills and wisdom. One of the great benefits of meeting confidentially with a group of peers is learning how much you don't know—month after month, year after year.

All too often, entrepreneurs are experts at one or two things, but they don't have a clue about the rest. Creating and growing a business requires a broad set of talents and skills. Those who dare to do it without plugging the holes in their skill sets are only increasing their already high odds of failure. Some of us learned this lesson the hard way, while others were lucky enough to make good hiring choices along the way. The smartest among us acknowledged our weaknesses at the outset and made sure we had a team in place whose talents made up for them, even before we launched our companies.

Over the course of Pete Settle's career, he came to recognize that he was not a happy administrator. "Everybody is defective in some way," he notes. "The best thing I did as a leader was finding people who could complement my weaknesses, which are many."[1] Pete managed his family's school bus company and then worked as a top executive for the large public company they sold it to. When he started his own company, the first thing he did was hire his older brother Mike as his chief operating officer.

"We have very complementary skill sets. I was the one who would go out and make promises to the clients about what we could do for them, and Mike would keep those promises." In 2012, Pete sold the company to the National Express Group, a British multinational transport company, which is now the number two provider of school bus services in North America. After a few years as CEO of National Express's North American transit operations, Pete tired of his administrative responsibilities and moved on. Mike stayed and is currently the senior vice president for the company's operations in Ohio, Pennsylvania, and Michigan.

Some people discover their talents as entrepreneurs and dealmakers when they join forces with people with very different skills. Take my old friend Richard Block, who graduated from college in the early 1960s and went to work for Westvaco (the Fortune 500 paper company). Richard became the youngest sales manager in the company's history, and in 1967 he was transferred to Chicago.[2] Months before returning to New York in 1970, Richard heard a rumor that a small printing company was about to acquire one of his biggest customers. A proactive salesman, he went to visit the small company to see what the real story was.

He met that company's cost estimator, Don Kosterka, and made a real connection. Don was well schooled in the printing business but didn't like the direction his company was going. Over subsequent meetings, he told Richard about the company he was planning to start, which would not only print record album jackets but design them too. He introduced Richard to his secret weapon, Jim Ladwig, a Grammy-nominated art director who was then at Mercury Records. A short while later, Don and Jim quit their jobs and launched Album Graphics Inc.

Six months later, Richard was back in New York settling into the next job on the ladder of Westvaco. But working for a big company had finally started to lose its appeal.

Back in Chicago, Don and Jim's new company was up and running, and they were ready for a sales partner. Their first choice was the genius who got Andy Warhol to work with the Rolling Stones on the jacket for their *Sticky Fingers* album, which was instantly iconic because it featured a real, working zipper on a photo of a pair of jeans. Their prospective partner overplayed his hand by asking for half the equity of the company. (No wonder you hear the expression, "Bulls make money, bears make money, but pigs get slaughtered.")

"Don was a manufacturing genius, and Jim was a creative genius," Richard says. Richard claims his own main achievements in college had been on the football field, but Don and Jim needed an ambitious young salesman to round out the partnership and Richard met all their expectations. Plus, he asked to earn only 15 percent of the equity out of future profits. It was early days at Album Graphics, but they made a pivotal deal with Polygram Records, and within three years Richard and his partners were producing album jackets for almost every other major label. Even though Richard was based in New York and his partners lived in Chicago, "We talked every day on the phone about everything," Richard recalls. "It was an incredible gearing of talents. We never got in each other's way."

"No printer offered high-quality design previously. That disrupted the business model," Richard continues. "The best-selling artists wanted to control their own album art, so they came to us." The trio's timing couldn't have been better. The British Invasion and the 1969 Woodstock Festival powered the music business into the next decade and beyond. Jim's stable of innovative art directors and designers appealed to the aesthetic tastes of many of the best-selling bands.

Seventeen exciting years passed. Don and Jim believed the company had reached its maximum growth potential, and they were ready to sell. Richard disagreed, so with the help of private equity investors and a big bank loan, he bought them out. Don sold 90 percent of his stock, and Jim sold all of his, but Richard stayed close to both of them. Jim had sold out, in part, because he thought the company needed to be managed from Chicago, and even though Richard promised to commute three days a week from New York, Jim thought it wasn't enough. Despite that, Jim stayed on as head designer, but with no equity exposure. Over the next 13 years, Jim and his team racked up another string of Grammy nominations and awards.

Growth always seems to create unexpected challenges. Most major artists released their big albums in the fall, which meant that for the first eight months of the year, Richard's factories were grossly underutilized. Being a great entrepreneur, Richard chose to see this problem as an opportunity. To utilize that excess capacity, he diversified into new contra-cyclical categories, printing high-quality packaging for liquor and cosmetic companies, such as Avon, L'Oréal, and Estee Lauder, during the first months of each year. At its peak, Richard's company, rebranded AGI, was running 17 printing plants (many adjacent to the major labels' record pressing plants and, later, their CD pressing plants). Getting there wasn't easy, and it was especially challenging to figure out how to lure really high-quality customers from completely different industries to balance the factory load throughout the year. It took almost a year to get a first sales visit to Avon, for example. At the time, Avon had nine suppliers in the category Richard was pitching business for. Seven years later there was just one, and it was AGI.

Under Richard's leadership after Richard's buyout of his original partners, sales went from $35 million in 1987 to $325 million in 2000. "I loved the company and didn't want to sell," Richard confesses now, noting that in the ensuing years he turned down multiple offers from one of the nation's biggest paper companies. But eventually, his investors and employee shareholders were ready. In 2000, Richard finally agreed to sell the company—to MeadWestvaco, the latest manifestation of the company he had worked for in the 1960s when he first met his partners.

Richard is a sensitive guy. To this day, it weighs heavily on him that Don and Jim didn't participate so much in that grand finale. Nonetheless, it was a point of deep pride to him that Don's 10 percent was worth more in 2000 at the time of the next sale than the 90 percent he'd sold in 1987.

And even though Don and Jim sold almost all their interests before the period when the most value was created, Richard gives his initial partners plenty of credit for that later success. "It might have never happened for me," Richard insists. "I believe the magic bullet was in the amazing synchronization between the three of us. Even after they dropped out, that quality of meshing for the common good at the company continued. It had become our DNA. Another astonishing thought is that had a simple spontaneous decision I made—to visit that little printer who was acquiring one of my customers—not been made, I would not have been part of this story."

That kind of magic is often available to entrepreneurs who surround themselves with people who are smarter than they are—or who at least have the skills that they themselves are short on.

Notes

1. Pete Settle, interview (June 15, 2015).
2. Richard Block, interview (December 11, 2012).

Diversity Makes
You Smarter

Many of Tiger 21's members join because they are searching for a safe haven in which to grapple with the uncertainties of their next act. They are deeply attracted to exploring the pros and cons of different opportunities and scenarios confidentially with economic peers who have enjoyed similar levels of success. They want to learn how others have dealt with their share of failure and success and how they have navigated such challenges over a lifetime. Most of us soon learn, however, that the ultimate benefit of a peer-to-peer group is not what you have in common but what's different about your backgrounds and business experiences.

In recent years, *diversity* has become a hollow, politically correct word. But real diversity is critically important. The pragmatic benefits that flow from having people with different backgrounds and expertise in a room have been backed up by decades of research by psychologists, organizational experts, and management gurus.

The evolution of our groups has certainly confirmed it. Among our members are Latinos, African Americans, East and South Asians, and Central Europeans. Our members exhibit a cross section of sexual preferences, populate most of the political spectrum, and represent any number of religious and nonreligious beliefs.

And while men still far outnumber women, as the number of highly successful female entrepreneurs has increased, more of them are turning to our organization for the same reasons that our male members do: to learn how

81

to preserve their wealth, deal with legacy issues, and find a confidential community of peers with whom they can share their ideas and receive honest, unbiased, and considerate feedback.

Diversity within our membership has had a noticeable effect on meetings. In one case reported to me, a member confided to his group that he was involved in such a brutal conflict with his brother that he was planning to exit their partnership. Other members began giving him advice about how to dissolve the partnership—until the women in the room interrupted. A competing consensus emerged, which one of the women later summed up as, "Wait a minute! This is your brother. He's family. Isn't there some way that this relationship can be repaired?" Suddenly, the conversation moved in a less combustible direction. In the words of one of the male members, "There was certainly a different kind of energy in that room today."

The idea that women, compared to men, tend to be more tuned in to the feelings of others and are likely to be more respectful in social and business situations is not new. It was certainly discussed in 1982, when then Harvard psychologist Carol Gilligan published a best-selling research report that showed that, from an early age, women approached moral responsibility "in a different voice."[1] This voice focuses on a concern for others and is more commonly used by women. It is an integral part of the *human voice* but tends to be overlooked. Gilligan observes that it is more common for many women's developmental paths to allow them to tap into universal values and emotions, so, although commonly misunderstood or mislabeled as a "woman's voice," Gilligan sees it as a universal voice that women more frequently access.

In 1990, Sally Helgesen wrote an equally classic book that argued that the different management styles of women executives gave businesses a "female advantage."[2] A 2010 study of what made for highly successful project teams found that a key difference was the emotional intelligence of the team—and the number of women, who turned out to be better readers of their colleagues.[3] Other recent studies have shown that the presence of women as well as ethnic and racial minorities in management inspires colleagues to think more critically and creatively, leading to better decision making and financial performance.[4]

But as beneficial as a broader sociocultural makeup can be to any group, what keeps teaching me and my fellow Tiger 21 members new lessons is diversity of *points of view.* "If you get a bunch of accountants in the room, I don't care if half of them are women," notes David Russell, a longtime Tiger 21 member, "they're going to come up with an accountant's point of view." I agree. In my experience, the meetings that really deliver powerful insights are those that have a wide range of expertise and experience in the room;

for example, somebody with a legal background, another with operational experience, a third with investment chops, and maybe a fourth who is a marketing expert—all from different industries. And the more gender and ethnic diversity, the better.

I can't count how many times a diversity of views has generated important questions that would have never been raised otherwise. One person may focus on the track record of an investment manager pitching his fund when another asks about turnover of the management team. Maybe a third person asks how much capital the management team has invested personally and what percent of their net worth that represents. A fourth wants to know if the general partner owns a second home or a yacht and how much time she is spending on distractions, including philanthropic activities, which might be great for society but could limit her focus on her business. When fund managers make a presentation to one of our groups that includes a member from the related industry (who might have even more experience or success than the presenter), sparks fly, insights pop up, and the group as a whole gets an education that no one on their own could duplicate. "You won't get that kind of insight watching one of the business networks," notes David.

And you won't get it if you only hire people who went to the same schools or nod at everything you say. Great entrepreneurs are innovators by definition; they always have an eye out for the next opportunity. Participating in diverse groups and assembling diverse teams inside your organization will make you and your company smarter, more creative, and more productive.

Notes

1. Carol Gilligan, *In a Different Voice* (Cambridge, MA: Harvard University Press, 1982).
2. Sally Helgesen, *The Female Advantage: Women's Ways of Leadership* (New York: Doubleday: 1990); Sally Helgesen and Julie Johnson, *The Female Vision: The Real Power of Women at Work* (San Francisco: Berrett-Koehler Publishers, 2010).
3. Anita Woolley, Thomas W. Malone, and Christopher Chabris, "Why Some Teams Are Smarter Than Others," *New York Times* (January 18, 2015). (The authors, who teach at Carnegie Mellon, MIT, and Union College, respectively, led the study cited here, originally published in the journal *Science*.)
4. See: Katherine Phillips, "How Diversity Makes Us Smarter," *Scientific American* (October 1, 2014); and Sheen S. Levine and David Stark, "Diversity Makes Us Smarter," *New York Times* (December 9, 2015). (Summary of their research study on the benefits of ethnic and racial diversity to groups.)

Risk Management

One of the variables that differentiate entrepreneurs from other business-people, indeed from most other humans, is their appetite for risk. It is often perceived to be unhealthy, even gluttonous. More often than not, a success-ful entrepreneur bets heavily—often against the odds—on one business: his own. Most people are *risk averse*; they'd rather be safe than sorry. Entrepre-neurs seem to seek out risk.

In his recent book, *Originals*, Adam Grant suggests entrepreneurs are actually *more* risk averse than others.[1] It clearly can't be that entrepreneurs are more risk averse *and* more risk seeking. I think this discrepancy reflects the different ways risk can be measured. I would suggest that by most con-ventional measures, the risks taken by successful entrepreneurs are great risks others would avoid. But in reality, because of the rare traits they bring to the table, many successful entrepreneurs analyze those risks differently and may envision unique ways to mitigate them. Other people simply may not have the creativity or intelligence to see these solutions. In that sense, successful entrepreneurs can be quite conservative because they do not take on risks that they are not confident they can effectively manage.

The act of walking away from a job or even a successful corporate career to start a business, often on savings or a loan or a credit card, is not for every-body. But as much as they feed on risk, the best entrepreneurs are not crazy risk-takers. They develop strategies—psychological as well as financial—to manage the kinds of risks that other people don't even consider. How can risk be quantified? The following lessons offer insights on how to assess and benefit from risk.

Note

1. Adam Grant, *Originals: How Non-Conformists Move the World* (New York: Penguin, 2016).

Risk Is in the Eye of the Beholder

In the standard economics textbooks, rational agents take risks only when the probability of a successful outcome exceeds a painful one. Of course, avoiding all risk—driving cars, playing sports, flying in planes, or living in cities, just to name a few everyday risky activities—would make for a dreary life. Uncertainty is one of the very few certain things in this world.

In fact, research shows that very smart people, including professional planners and decision makers, systematically underestimate risks all the time. As I noted earlier, the problem of optimism bias is so common among managers and entrepreneurs that the Nobel Prize winner Daniel Kahneman and his late partner Amos Tversky came up with a name for it: *planning fallacy*. "In its grip," Kahneman writes, "they make decisions based on delusional optimism rather than on a rational weighting of gains, losses, and probabilities."[1]

The psychologists are right in one sense. Entrepreneurs are not looking at risk accurately because their high levels of optimism let them underprice risk and move forward. It seems probable to me that this is genetically coded. Without optimism bias, ancient humans would not have risked their lives to hunt the woolly mammoths or bears that fed the tribe. High levels of somewhat unjustified optimism seem to be most prevalent in 20-to-30-year-old men.[2,3] Perhaps this is why they are more likely than others to choose—and claim to enjoy—jobs that are full of stress and risk, like flying fighter jets, trading commodities, and working on oil rigs.

But where the psychologists go wrong is getting too hung up on the role of *rational weighting* and *probabilities*, which presume that risks can be accurately appraised. My own experience, which matches the experiences of a number of entrepreneurs, has convinced me that risk can be in the eye of the beholder.

For example, let's say I've spent 25 years in the real estate business and you've spent 25 years in an entirely different industry, and we're both looking at the same building. Both of us agree that it has problems. Perhaps it's a bit dilapidated or on the wrong side of the tracks. But my 25 years have shown me paths for creating value that you can't see. For me, the risk might seem dramatically lower than it does to you—and the potential upside leverage that much greater. I'm not saying that experienced entrepreneurs are omniscient and should always trust their guts, and that the analysts who quantify risk are always blind. That would be stupid. But I think that it's equally stupid to believe that there is only one way to weigh risk.

What mitigates the uncertainty in any deal or investment can be your expertise or unique perspective. That badly located building could be a very good deal if the price is cheap enough, and I can see a new use for it that might not occur to you.

As my mentor David Fromer taught me, "There is no such thing as good or bad real estate, just good and bad deals." That perspective doesn't apply only to real estate.

I was reminded of the profundity of David's insight while reading Howard Marks's 2011 book on investing, *The Most Important Thing: Uncommon Sense for the Thoughtful Investor*, which has already become a classic. "High risk," Marks explains, "comes primarily with high prices," no matter how diversified your investments are or how accurately you have measured volatility in the markets.[4]

But how do you know when you're paying too much? As you saw in the previous lesson, if the opportunity you are considering is in real estate, it helps to have the experienced eye of a successful real estate entrepreneur. As naturally optimistic and comfortable with risk-taking as they are, the best entrepreneurs I know are risk averse in one clear way: They are not likely to pursue opportunities that are outside their expertise. And if they do, they are highly focused on learning enough of the fundamental dynamics of an opportunity to know what real value looks like.

Take David Russell. He advises, "If you're successful at something—real estate or software or whatever your expertise is—there's no particular reason to take on risk regarding things that you're not familiar with."[5] But David, a self-described *riskaholic*, has made himself successful at a dizzying variety of things. And he's done it by soaking up knowledge wherever he can find it.

David founded a communications software company that developed a proprietary delivery network for up-to-the-minute bond market information for banks and brokerage houses, which he sold in 1995 to Thomson Financial (now Thomson/Reuters). "When I sold my business, I didn't know anything about investing," he confesses. But David is a brilliant guy, a dedicated pianist, and an avid student of poetry who, with the advice of fellow entrepreneurs, turned himself into a pro. Now he is in the energy business, investing in technologies to recover oil and gas cheaply.

In August 2015, when the price of oil had plummeted from $107 the year before to $39 a barrel, David reported that he had millions of dollars invested in his own oil company—and was planning to invest significantly more at year's end. He was betting that prices would still be low, leaving those who borrowed to buy oil at $60 plus "in pain" as the banks recalled their loans. "This will be the best time in perhaps a generation to buy oil assets, so that's what I'm doing. As I said, I'm a riskaholic."

David's confidence is based on considerable knowledge about the business he's in. And not only that, he believes he has an edge based on price. The technology that his oil company has developed can get a barrel of oil out of the ground and to the refinery for less than $10, which means that it's possible to make a profit whether oil is selling for $30, $45, or $100-plus. I sure hope he is right, for his sake. Managing risk and eliminating it are very different things, and no matter how smart David is, the oil trade has a lot of risk.

Bottom line: Fear risk and respect your capacity for worry, but when you know your business and pricing is on your side, what looks like risk to everyone else can be a beautiful thing. That is the essence of an *edge*.

Notes

1. Daniel Kahneman, *Thinking, Fast and Slow* (New York: Farrar, Straus and Giroux, 2011), 252.
2. See: Noah Smith, "What Drives Men to Take Bigger Risks?" Bloomberg View, (September 24, 2015), and Francesco D'Acunto, "Why Are Men More Likely to Take Financial Risks?" World Economic Forum (September 23, 2015), https://www.weforum.org/agenda/2015/09/why-are-men-more-likely-to-take-financial-risks.

3. Jessica Firger, "Why Teenage Boys Do Stupid Things," CBS News (June 12, 2014), http://www.cbsnews.com/news/whats-wrong-with-the-teen-brain.
4. Howard Marks, *The Most Important Thing: Uncommon Sense for the Thoughtful Investor* (New York: Columbia Business School Publishing, 2011), 46.
5. David Russell, interview (August 28, 2015).

LESSON 17

Approach Risk Like a Farmer

You will not get this kind of advice in the *Wall Street Journal* or on CNBC. Honestly, it's a new take on risk for me, and I have thought about risk as much as I've thought about anything. I owe this lesson to Will Ade, the oil wildcatter you met in Lesson 3, who grew up on a farm in Indiana. "Nobody knows risk better than a farmer," says Will. "No hedge fund manager, no day trader, nobody: Crop prices go up or go down; it rains, or it doesn't rain; disease and pestilence in the crops. Every day you deal with risk growing up on the farm."[1]

Will's cool attitude toward risk has helped him see investment opportunities when just about everyone else is running for the hills. His first major score came in the early 1980s, when he was living in Brunei. His father called with some very bad news for a farm family. "The banks aren't lending me money anymore," his father told him. Will continued, "He gave me a first-hand description of the Great Farm Recession of the 1980s."

The roots of the crisis went back to the early 1970s, when the prices of agricultural commodities spiked after the U.S. negotiated a multiyear contract with the Soviet Union for wheat and feed grains. Between 1972 and 1974, the price of corn tripled; wheat prices doubled. Predictably, farmers borrowed money to ramp up production. As rural America thrived in 1973 and 1974, so did inflation, thanks to a rapid rise in oil prices due to the infamous Arab oil embargo in October 1973. Suddenly, the price of oil quadrupled (from $3 a barrel to $12), which led to a full-blown energy crisis in 1979 when the Iranian revolution overthrew the shah. To tamp down a double-digit rise in prices across the economy, the Federal Reserve Bank jacked up interest rates.

Then, in 1980, the Russians invaded Afghanistan, prompting President Jimmy Carter to place an embargo on grain shipments to the USSR. The result was a double whammy for rural America. Without access to the Russian market, feed grains piled up again and prices fell. By 1981, the prime interest rate had risen to 21.5 percent, still the all-time record, sending the U.S. economy into reverse gear. Net farm income declined by about 30 percent in 1985; land values fell 50 percent. One out of every three commercial-size farms was unable to pay its bills. All over the Midwest, banks were foreclosing.

"After that phone call with Dad," Will says, "I liquidated everything I had and started buying Indiana farmland at $1,000 [per] acre. Today, depending on whom you listen to, the same land is now worth about $8,000 to $10,000 an acre. Plus it pays a very nice dividend in cash rent." Will ended up buying six Indiana farms, including his father's.

It was a bold move in the middle of a recession that many commentators at the time were calling "the worst since the Great Depression." Will, however, had two advantages for assessing the risks. The farm boy in him knew that when the economy began growing again, so would demand for agricultural commodities and farmland; and as an oil man, he was used to volatility. More than three decades later, when the 2007–2008 financial crisis evolved into the latest titleholder for "worst recession since the Great Depression," Will was able to view that crisis as yet another investment opportunity.

By then, Will was living mainly off the royalties from his oil wells and the rents from his Indiana farmland, dividing the time he spent in the United States between his homes in Florida and Indiana. Eager to become a better and more diversified investor, he had joined Tiger 21 in Miami just weeks before credit markets froze, sending equities markets into free fall.

Few American investors escaped the carnage. The net worth of some of the members Will had just met plummeted by 20 percent or more. In March 2009, he was back in Indiana, meeting his Merrill Lynch stockbroker for lunch. "He didn't look well," Will recalls. The broker lamented that clients had been pulling their money out for months. Will assured him that things weren't any better in Florida, and then, with one sentence, he made his broker's day. "After lunch I want you to margin my account and start buying stocks." Will explains: "I took the reaction from the Tiger 21 members and what was going on with my broker in Indiana as the biggest buy signal of my life."

When the indices started rising again a year later, Will was already "100 percent invested" and well positioned to ride what turned out to be a very persistent bull market for the next six years. By the time I interviewed him in the late summer of 2015, he reported that he was "20 percent cash for the first time in my life," prepared to start buying when the bull market ended. Six months later, when oil prices had plummeted to a 12-year low of $27 in early 2016 and the stock markets had their worst starts since 1930, I checked in to see how he was doing. "A normal commodity cycle," said Will, punctuating that explanation of the collapse in oil prices with a big smile. He had sold his biggest energy position the previous July—for a 150 percent profit— and was waiting for another buy signal.

"Everyone faces risk every day," Will says. "Do you want to hide under your bed? A comet's going to smash you. You want to drive on the interstate, some lunatic's going to smash you. There's no way in life not to deal with risk. You have to embrace it."

Note

1. Will Ade, interviews (February 19 and August 14, 2015).

LESSON 18

Identify Your Blind Spots with a Periodic Portfolio Defense

In a 2010 *New York Times* story about Tiger 21, one of our members noted, "We all learn from each other; that's the magic of the place."

The source of much of that magic is the Portfolio Defense (PD), our signature feature. Just about every monthly meeting includes a PD, as we call the grilling that each of us must undergo every year on the critical and often emotional choices we have made in our financial lives. Members often prepare for days or weeks in advance, and the actual defense usually lasts for 90 minutes, no holds barred, and covers every stock, bond, private investment, fund position, and piece of real estate we own—and in some cases, our philanthropic interests. As important as the numbers are in isolation, they come to life when members share their answers to a detailed set of questions about their goals, personal life, family, and their anxieties about protecting their wealth and transferring it to children and charities. More broadly, the questions force our members to explore the broader meaning of wealth in their lives, and in what ways it can be used to lever philanthropic, political, or family goals and interests.

I have been doing an annual Portfolio Defense for 18 years. Yet I still enter the room with a combination of trepidation and curiosity regarding what the response to the latest report on the State of Sonnenfeldt will be.

Frankly, not everyone can handle such naked exposure. "I've seen people quit the group the week before their first Portfolio Defense, even the night before," a longtime member reports. "They just couldn't face the scrutiny."

That's their loss. The truth can hurt, but it also helps. I remember one PD in the late 1990s in which a member had allocated 40 percent of his portfolio to biotech stocks. None of us in that room pretended to be experts in biotech, but we knew from experience that falling in love with one sector of the economy as a passive investor was asking for trouble. At the end of the PD, the message could not have been clearer: reduce your exposure to biotech.

But he procrastinated. Although he had made his money in an unrelated field, he was now convinced that biotech was the future. It wasn't until a couple weeks before his next PD, the following year, that he began cutting back on his biotech shares. He later confessed that he didn't want to show up having done nothing.

Another memorable PD a decade ago revealed that the member had 75 percent of his assets invested in just one fund. Though everyone agreed that its returns were excellent, the consensus was that putting more than half of his assets in a single fund was way too risky. (Personally, having anything remotely close to half of that 75 percent in a single allocation would scare the bejesus out of me.) The member conceded the risks but insisted that the returns were simply too rich to pass up. He quit the group shortly thereafter. He didn't feel the advice his group had provided him was wise or useful. He had no interest in pulling his money out of a fund run by one of the top traders in the United States—Bernie Madoff.

Although Bernie Madoff was a well-known figure in New York investment circles, none of us knew at the time that he was operating the biggest Ponzi scheme in history, which, when it collapsed in 2008, destroyed billions of dollars of investors' assets. That ex-member's losses were grievous, but there were even more troubling stories of people so enamored with Madoff that they had actually mortgaged their apartments and invested the proceeds, effectively having put over 100 percent of their net worth at risk.

What that member didn't seem to realize was that, in Tiger 21, he had a "personal board of directors" on his side, as Charlie Garcia, the chair of multiple groups in South Florida, has dubbed the benefit of membership.[1] "I'm chairing the board," he explains. "There are 14 other members in the room who are very successful in different industries—from lawyers and bankers to hedge fund and private entrepreneurs—who also bring their investment, business, personal, and family challenges to the table."

One of the things that every member learns quickly is that no matter how smart or rich we might be, we all have our blind spots, If you don't know what they are, someone in your group will likely point them out to you. We try to soften the blows by encouraging a *care-frontational* approach. Still, even the kindest criticism from a world-class investor can make a world-class entrepreneur feel like a C student or worse. Part of my own anxiety about PDs is that, as the organization's founder, I feel like I should be a better investor than I am.

As I prepared for my PD at the end of 2013, however, I felt I was on the right track. The equity markets were ascending again, and I had followed my group's advice by hiring a full-time investment manager to join my team to help me manage my portfolio. I had also initiated a disciplined approach that the younger me would have hardly recognized. I'd jettisoned small holdings and sold off a house I'd been maintaining for sentimental reasons. I had devoted 20 percent of my time, with discipline, to managing my portfolio, brought on a full-time professional to help me professionalize our shop, and I was proud of the progress I'd made. I was expecting my fellow members to shower me with praise. The opposite happened.

Once all my non–real estate holdings were added up, the total value of my investment portfolio had risen by a mere 6.6 percent in a bullish year when the S&P 500 Index was up 40 percent. A member who heads a wealth management firm was horrified that 20 percent of my portfolio was in cash. My explanation: Even though my days of keeping cash on hand to finance my next big deal were over, I also looked at cash as a hedge against an unexpected disaster—a black-swan event like the 9/11 attacks, market crashes, or environmental catastrophes. I've never forgotten how relieved I was during the stock market crash of October 1987 to still be sitting on the proceeds of the sale of my first company in cash while everyone around me was in a panic.

One financier in the group zeroed in on the long equities in my portfolio, which had risen by only 1 percent. "If you had your money in muni bonds, tax-free, you'd get a better return sleeping," he advised. "Based on your performance, I'd fire the manager, which would be you." He was right. I don't pick individual stocks anymore.

Then one of my oldest friends in the group pointed out that the financial successes I had cited in my report were minor. "You've gone from a D to a C minus," he said. "If you're spending 20 percent of your time managing this money, you've really got a problem. This is not the right pursuit for you." Another member, who had been vice chairman of a major Wall Street investment firm, said he thought I should keep whittling down the positions in the portfolio, from 77 to 40, maybe even 30. "The smallest position should be worth 2 percent of the total; the largest around 8 percent."

After 90 minutes, I had heard a lot of expert opinions and investment suggestions. One of my most useful takeaways from that PD was a bit of self-knowledge that has made me a more mature investor today. I've finally accepted that I am not likely to ever measure up to the world-class investors in our organization. My solution has been to negotiate a compromise between being an active entrepreneur, always on the lookout for great opportunities for exciting returns, and being a passive investor intent on protecting his wealth. Both sides seem content, at least for now.

Most comforting of all is that I have such a large, wise personal board of directors on hand—fellow members whose only interest in my portfolio is my well-being. Whenever a major decision emerges in my life about business, investments, philanthropy, and even family concerns, I have trained myself to ask, "Who in Tiger 21 can give me the best counsel on this?"

What are your blind spots? If you don't have an answer (or believe you have none), you need to assemble your own personal board of directors to help you evaluate how well you're managing your business, your money, and your personal life. As Charlie Garcia notes, "In order for you to live an authentic life or be an authentic leader, you need to surround yourself with people who will give you their honest feedback."

One note: I can't count the number of times a friend or an acquaintance has come to me for advice on a small business they own or are contemplating acquiring or creating. Inevitably I ask, "Do you have a board of directors?" Shockingly (to me anyway), most respond that they hadn't even thought of that. In almost every case where I was able to convince the person to recruit and empower a board, it has been an unqualified success. Everyone has blind spots. Having decent, honorable, committed, and wise advisors is one of the greatest tools any entrepreneur can have.

Note

1. Charlie Garcia, interview (July 29, 2015).

STAGE 4

Growing Your Business the Smart Way

One reason so many entrepreneurs fail is that there is no playbook for building a company. "You do what it takes" is a common refrain among our entrepreneurs. Many had the feeling of making it up along the way as they dealt with one crisis or another. Another common description of the entrepreneurial challenge: "It's like building a bicycle while riding it."

Company builders learn the benefits of quick decisions and often survive by improvisation. "You're making decisions every day—yes, no, no, yes," explains one Tiger 21 member. "Overanalyzing can get in the way." The best entrepreneurs even think differently than corporate managers. This section offers insights on how entrepreneurs can nurture their creative thinking while leading their team to success.

LESSON 19

Entrepreneurship Is Rarely about Just Making Money

In 2014, Barbara Roberts, a serial entrepreneur and the first woman on the board of financial services firm Dean Witter (which was later acquired by Morgan Stanley), researched and wrote "The Owner's Journey," a Columbia University Business School white paper, featuring eight case studies of entrepreneurs who had sold their businesses or transferred them to family members. I read Barbara's report with interest, especially when I came across this insight:

> Few entrepreneurs start companies with the sole goal of getting rich. Often, they launch companies to fix a problem, to create something new, to act upon an insight that only they see, or even simply to make the world a better place.[1]

That certainly describes my own experience. As grueling as it was to get my first enterprise off the ground, I loved the work of revitalizing a forgotten stretch of the urban landscape where I saw the potential of a revitalized Jersey City waterfront long before other much more experienced developers and government planners did. During the years I ran the development, I almost never thought about cashing out, and I only reluctantly agreed to sell when forced by my partner with few other viable choices. What most people do not understand is that while money is at the heart of business, it's far from the sole motivation. What drives many entrepreneurs is the urge to build something, create something totally new, to turn around a wreck, or even to change the world for the better, as more than a few of the members of our organization have done with their philanthropies and impact investments.

Barbara, however, added, "In many ways, entrepreneurs are like artists, bringing huge passion to what they are doing and creating."[2] *Artists!?* That seemed a bit much to me. As an amateur photographer and sometime art collector, I was reluctant to compare what I do as an entrepreneur to what fine artists do. Barbara, however, who serves as "entrepreneur-in-residence" at Columbia Business School, pressed this point. "I believe that entrepreneurs are like Van Gogh," she likes to say. "When he painted 'Starry Night,' he wasn't thinking of the final sale price. He just painted what he was driven to paint." It's a point that resonates with Barbara's students. "Passion and purpose are the secrets to entrepreneurship," she notes in one of her lectures. "If entrepreneurs were focused only on creating value and selling companies, they would make different decisions."

Barbara's analogy between the artist and the entrepreneur began to resonate with me as I talked to more entrepreneurs about their careers and reflected on my own trajectory. When an entrepreneur like Robert Oringer says, "There's something about startups that I love—something about creating new things that no one else has done,"[3] it's hard not to hear an echo of that historic slogan of modern art: "Make it new!" The art of entrepreneurship also captures the continual creative struggle of building a valuable business. While CEOs manage companies and investors bankroll them, we entrepreneurs *create* them out of nothing more than an idea.

While Robert is no more inclined to call himself an artist than I am, over the past two decades he has created an impressive number of new businesses. As you may recall from Lesson 7, his motivation comes from a desire to solve the problems faced by people living with diabetes and their families, starting with his own children. He is, however, quite forthright about his passion for entrepreneurship, which blossomed during his freshman year at the University of Pennsylvania's Wharton School in 1979, when he launched a successful T-shirt business capitalizing on the Penn basketball team's surprise advance to the Final Four of the NCAA tournament.

After putting in nearly five years as an award-winning salesman at IBM, Robert bought a small business importing biofeedback instruments into Canada. To finance the purchase, he used cash wedding gifts combined with a loan from his father-in-law. Two years later, he merged it with AMG

Medical, a successful Montreal medical supply company run by two partners who, according to Robert, "were looking for a smart kid who could sell and knew computers and could help them grow their business."

Robert, a one-third partner, did just that, and then launched several more businesses. "I was not the operating guy," he notes. "My great partners allowed me to focus on strategy and vision—and painting a picture of that vision." Eager to get into the American market, Robert led a sister company, CanAm Care, which became a pioneer in producing private-label lancets, syringes, and other diabetes care products for local wholesale and retail pharmacies in the United States who were eager to build their own brands. Robert is also the creator of the popular over-the-counter Dex4 brand of glucose tablets used for treating mild or moderate episodes of hypoglycemia.

In 1998, he sold CanAm Care to Inverness Medical Technology, a major U.S. innovator in diagnostic devices, such as home pregnancy tests and glucose monitors. When Johnson & Johnson acquired Inverness's diabetes assets in 2001, Robert bought his old company back from them—and then sold it again in 2014 for $36 million.

In 2009, he launched yet another diabetes-focused venture, Locemia Solutions, whose mission was to create a rescue method for severe episodes of hypoglycemia that is needle-free, injection-free, and insanely simple to teach. "The risk of severe hypoglycemia hangs over insulin users and their families all the time," Robert explains. Diabetics can quickly become disoriented or even unconscious if their blood-sugar level drops. Historically, the remedy has been to get glucagon into the patient's system through an extremely complicated rescue kit. These kits require a caregiver to open a container, remove a liquid-filled syringe, inject the liquid into a vial of glucagon powder, shake it, draw the liquid back into the syringe, and then inject it into the hypoglycemic person. All the while, the clock is ticking.

In 2015, Locemia presented its breakthrough at a major diabetes technology conference. The delivery device easily pumps a puff of a proprietary glucagon powder formulation into the victim's nose, where it is quickly absorbed by the nasal mucosa into the blood. The product was so impressive that by the end of the year, even though the device had not completed the FDA-required clinical trials, the pharmaceutical giant Eli Lilly had bought the worldwide rights to it with the intention of launching it to eventually replace their own product, which is currently the market leader.

Robert is an active angel investor in new diabetes-related ventures, including the company that launched the first blood glucose meter that plugged directly into the iPhone. He has never stopped searching for the next breakthrough. "I love creating companies from scratch, and the challenge of figuring out strategy and the ever-morphing, multidimensional puzzle that all startup founders live with," he says, sounding like an artist again.

Robert's story points to another essential variable in the art of the entrepreneur: the capacity to improvise. Recently, I had lunch with the attorney who represented David Fromer and me when we were developing the Harborside Terminal in the early 1980s. Reminiscing about the young and green entrepreneur I was at age 25 reminded me how much I had to depend on my creative instincts to keep moving forward. This was not about going into a garage to make a widget that I could sell. Turning an old waterfront terminal into the nation's largest commercial renovation put us in a danger zone where unions and politics face off New Jersey–style. I immersed myself in the subtleties of the legal issues surrounding waterfront development to the point where I could often go toe to toe with the lawyers in the room. And dealing with the unions that controlled the loading docks was right out of a movie, one that pitted the son of an engineer and a social worker, raised in the sheltered suburbs of Long Island, against some very tough guys. Some bad apples in the union dockhands who unloaded the trucks and delivered the merchandise to the tenants on the terminal's upper floors were inclined to steal a fraction of whatever passed across the loading dock. If we were going to convert the old warehouse into a modern office building, we needed to wrest control of the loading docks from the union and find a way to stanch our tenants' losses.

Initially, all the upper floors were served by shared ground-floor loading docks where supplies, machines, and shipments for each tenant were loaded in and out. Our solution was to carve up the docks into individual spaces so that each major tenant could have its own elevator and private loading dock manned by its own people. In return for reducing the number of union jobs, we offered lifetime contracts for some of the existing laborers. That was the price we were willing to pay. The union told us to stuff it.

The warehouse, which was the equivalent in size to 80 floors of one of the original World Trade Center towers, was heated by huge oil-fired boilers that consumed truckloads of oil every week of the heating season. The hammer that the union had over us was that their contract always ended in January— at the peak of the heating season. If the union went on strike, the oil trucks wouldn't be able to cross the picket lines to fill the tanks. The union knew that shutting down the building was a thousand times more expensive than giving the dockhands a raise.

My solution was to begin converting the building to gas-fired heaters, essentially repiping the entire 2-million-square-foot building. Eventually, no more oil truck deliveries would need to cross the picket lines, and gas would be piped in. But to reduce the potential for violence until the gas system was in place, I arranged for our heating oil to be shipped in by barge from the river-facing side of our waterfront building. There were still threats of violence, and one oil truck driver was roughed up before we could fully cross over to riverside deliveries. But legally, we controlled the waterside. My next move was to bring in guards and station cameramen on the roof, so that if the union tried to stop the barge or rough up any more drivers, I could bring them before the National Labor Relations Board and show the film of their contract violations.

Another Van Gogh? Hardly, though I was definitely possessed by a passion to succeed that was equal to the most intense of artists. Juggling so many variables en route to creating the most valuable private commercial office/mixed-use complex in the state of New Jersey out of a warehouse in serious decline may not be *Art with a capital A*, but it does involve a great deal of seat-of-the-pants artistry.

Notes

1. Barbara Roberts, Murray B. Low, Brian Thomas, Keith Banks, and Mitchell A. Drossman, "The Owner's Journey," Columbia Business School and U.S. Trust (May 2015).
2. Barbara Roberts, interview (August 5, 2015).
3. Robert Oringer, interview (July 21, 2016).

Hone Three Different Kinds of Focus

One of the most obvious talents I've detected among the best entrepreneurs—those who've created billion-dollar companies from scratch, and then done it again—is their ability to focus, which can be monomaniacal in almost a scary kind of way. "Obsessive business focus" was the term used by the authors of a 2015 UBS/PwC report on billionaires: "After they have identified [a new business] opportunity, they switch to an extremely focused modus operandi in execution that some observers could call 'tunnel vision.'"[1]

I've created a number of businesses and have certainly experienced periods of intense focus in my life. Others appear to sustain that focus for far longer, sometimes decades, and achieve success of another order of magnitude. Nonstop, obsessive focus? I suspect I only experienced that between the ages of 25 and 30 when I was developing Harborside, which provided the greatest relative increase of wealth in my career, mainly because I started with almost zero net worth. (Note: This is not a complaint because, admittedly, I had many advantages that others do not in education and background and potential support if I ran into trouble.)

Oddly enough, there is a great paradox, which perhaps reflects the unique nature of entrepreneurs. On the one hand, entrepreneurs frequently have endless energy and suffer from attention deficit disorder (ADD) that keeps them going in so many directions, often at once or in rapid-fire succession. On the other hand, despite their predisposition to easy distraction, one of the key traits of so many successful entrepreneurs is their ability to sustain laser-like focus for as long as it takes to achieve success.

I've always wondered what it takes to harness that kind of intense focus over sustained periods of time and whether it can be learned. In recent years, neuroscientists have done a great deal of research in the area of attention, some of it covered in the 2013 book *Focus: The Hidden Driver of Excellence*, by Daniel Goleman, a psychologist who popularized the early research on emotional intelligence. Focus is indeed an important factor in success, not just for businesspeople but also for those who excel in sports, education, and the arts. The science of attention reveals that the kind of focus these high performers display is no blunt instrument but a many-splendored faculty. The most successful business leaders have, as Goleman puts it, "a triple focus."[2] This triple focus includes: 1) *inner focus* (self-awareness of their strengths and weaknesses); 2) *other focus* (attending to the needs of people around them, particularly their employees and customers); and 3) *outer focus* (keeping an eye on what's happening in the world that might require a change in business strategy or even a rethinking of the entire business model).

Such triple focus is so much more than tunnel vision, which comes as a relief to me. It was nice to learn that my political and social interests and my general curiosity about new ideas and technologies count as a better kind of focus, which, as I look back on my checkered career, must have helped keep me on track.

Neal Milch is a textbook example of someone with a high-performing, multifocused brain. "I'm incredibly persistent," explains Neal, who runs Laundrylux, a leader in the commercial laundry business for more than 60 years.[3] "You have to be able to go to superhuman lengths to survive—to be able to act even when you have nothing in your pocket. I had nothing but my willpower." What Neal didn't realize was that what he calls "willpower" is much more than mere self-control or even grit, but precisely the kind of multidimensional focus that distinguishes the most talented entrepreneurs.

Neal's father, Bernie Milch, pioneered the coin-operated laundry business, parlaying a rare combination of technical know-how and a genius for marketing into a virtual 25-year hammerlock on the North American distribution of the durable, energy-efficient commercial washing machines made by the Swedish company Wascator. As a young Holocaust refugee, Bernie earned his living in postwar New York City as a machinery repairman, but he soon found a niche fixing laundry equipment for hotels, commercial laundries, and local wash-and-fold services. His big break came in 1956 when an insurance company hired him to evaluate the damage to the laundry room of the Swedish passenger ship the *Stockholm*. Off Nantucket, the *Stockholm* had survived a collision with the Italian cruise ship *Andrea Doria*, which sank.

Neal's father entered the *Stockholm*'s dried-out laundry room assuming that the saltwater had destroyed the washing machines, but when he turned on the power, they all were in working order. "He was astounded," says Neal, adding: "We like to imagine that a shaft of light from the heavens penetrated the hold, and little cherubs fluttered their wings and said, 'Bernie, Bernie, this is the washing machine! This is the washing machine!'"

The plate on the back of the washers revealed the brand to be Wascator, which Bernie traced to the small city of Kungsbacka, Sweden. After writing twice to the company and receiving no reply, Bernie borrowed some money, traveled to Sweden on a freighter, and imported a Wascator washer. Back in New York, he dismantled it, figured out how to attach a coin meter and moneybox, and then tested its durability and wash results, confirming that the Swedish front-loading stainless-steel commercial washers were superior to the top-loaders favored by U.S. laundries.

In 1958, he finally persuaded Wascator to award him the sales and marketing rights to their machines in North America, and he then proceeded to go door to door to coin-operated laundries in New York City, talking the owners into installing his Swedish machines, splitting the accumulated quarters two times a week. According to Neal, it wasn't long before an owner would say, "I don't want you as a partner. I'll buy the washer, and I want more. My customers love them!"

That was the beginning of a company that revolutionized the North American coin-operated laundry industry, which Bernie named Wascomat, combining the Swedish brand name and his favorite lunch spot in Manhattan, the legendary Automat, where an immigrant whose English was still a work in progress could eat without having to cope with menus or waitresses. This European refugee had a very American dream. "He saw that in post–World War II America times were going to be good, people were going to have families, and this concept of a professional self-service laundry was going to take off," notes Neal. "And he was right."

Bernie eventually started lending money to customers with Italian, Greek, and Hispanic names—immigrant entrepreneurs like himself who had no chance of getting a loan from a bank. He gradually developed a finance branch of the company, the first in the industry. As the sole distributor of washing machines strong enough to withstand a shipwreck, Wascomat gained an impressive share of the self-service coin laundry and commercial laundry market in North America, marketing the "well-built Swede" washing machines to hotels, motels, nursing homes, hospitals, and other on-premises laundry operations, including Polaris nuclear submarines.

"We had a monopoly on this kind of commercial laundry equipment for about 25 years," marvels Neal, "earning monopoly profits." In 1973, Bernie arranged for Electrolux, a Swedish appliance manufacturer with a large business in domestic laundry equipment, to acquire Wascator and invest in product development.

Neal, who had worked at Wascomat during summers since he was a little kid, always figured he'd eventually work for the family company, unlike his brother who went to medical school and pursued other interests. In 1985, after graduating from Stanford University and Columbia Law School and practicing law for two years, Neal began working full time for Wascomat's finance operation. It was not fun. According to Neal, his father was an "autocrat" who didn't want anyone questioning his decisions or suggesting different ways of doing business. "Let's just say we knocked heads more than a few times," he says.

For 16 years, in fact. "He was constantly undermining what I was doing, putting me down in public." Why did Neal take the abuse? "I had invested many years in the company," explains Neal, "and I had seen my predictions come true and my instincts validated. I knew that I knew what I was doing." Neal also realized that he had inherited his father's entrepreneurial genes. He was noticing a new and more tech-savvy cohort entering the coin-operated laundry business who wanted to have programming flexibility with their machines. "My father said it would never work—probably because he didn't understand and had no interest understanding." Without his father's knowledge, Neal worked with Electrolux's research and development engineers to develop a microprocessor-controlled, coin-operated washing machine. He designed the user interface, the programs, and even the graphics of the control manual. "I also wrote the user manual and all the marketing material for my Emerald Series washers," he recalls. "I then bought a container load of these new computerized washers and built a coin-op laundry featuring them in New Jersey, and sales took off like a rocket."

Despite the Emerald Series' success nationwide and internationally, Bernie never acknowledged the success and even denied that Neal had anything to do with the project. In 2001, Neal finally quit. "My dad was just impossible to deal with and was obviously threatened by my success and growing reputation." By the end of 2002, Neal had moved his family to Copenhagen because Electrolux had hired him as head of global marketing. He was tasked with helping to shift the company in "a more entrepreneurial direction," meeting the needs of customers instead of just building what the engineers wanted.

As he immersed himself over the next two years in the Electrolux culture and their customer-focused product development, he was getting periodic reports from Wascomat employees about his father's erratic behavior. More bothersome, however, was that "my father was driving the business into the ground" while a competitor was growing with the help of private equity investments and treating its distributors better. Neal recalls that the competition was doing "all the stuff I had wanted to do but didn't have the power to."

Frustrated over Bernie's business stagnation and increasingly unprofessional behavior, Electrolux canceled his contract and offered to buy the company "for half of what it was worth," according to Neal, who returned to the United States better prepared to run the business than ever. First, however, he had to make sure his father didn't sell the company precipitously.

At his father's request, Neal turned to his legal training and got involved in the negotiations with Electrolux. Dealing with his father daily, he realized that Bernie was suffering from dementialike symptoms. Electrolux soon figured out that Neal was actively undermining the acquisition, and the negotiations collapsed in rancor. Neal pivoted to try to patch up the business. When Electrolux sweetened its offer a year later, Neal jumped back into the negotiations, once again preventing a sale to give him enough time to revamp the company. "I'm losing weight, I'm not sleeping, facing this sort of extinction-level event," he recalls of that period. Once again, Neal managed to sabotage the deal, but the situation was far from good. Morale had plummeted among his employees and distributors. Electrolux hated him. His father had retreated into angry solitude. Neal appealed to his mother and brother, who refused to intercede with his father and considered it a lost cause. "The whole thing was a disaster," he recalls. To top it all off, Neal's wife was diagnosed with breast cancer and was undergoing radiation and chemotherapy treatment, adding to the family's stress.

The only thing Neal had on his side was time. As Electrolux's biggest commercial laundry customer, his father had managed years earlier to negotiate a contract that would keep the Swedish machines coming for seven years after the agreement was canceled. Neal turned his focus to the wrenching necessity of removing his father from power. He hired guards to prevent him from entering the building; he even dismantled his office down to bare walls and floors, cutting power and phone lines. As family, friends, and lawyers all predicted, his father threatened to sue him, even kill him—for three weeks. And then, according to Neal, "He collapsed mentally. It was over. I had finally won, but I had a huge mess on my hands with a contract that was expiring in three years, like a ticking bomb."

In 2007, Neal took over the company only to realize, "There's no one here to help me. I have to save it." He informed the family's banker and investment advisors—all of whom had been troubled by his father's erratic behavior—that he was now fully in charge. It took him more than a year to gain control of all the bank accounts related to the business. Electrolux, which owned the Wascator name, sued in federal court for trademark infringement related to the use of the Wascomat mark. Neal put his law degree to use again, this time to assist his lawyers in the case. He was "working until midnight every day of the week," only to lose the trademark lawsuit but actually win the war. "I was so intensely focused on discovering evidence and I provided the lawyers with so much background information that we nearly overturned their trademark, which Electrolux hadn't supervised properly." Nor was Electrolux prepared for Neal's intense defense, spending five times more than he spent on legal fees. "It smashed their quarterly results. And I fully intended to appeal!" That financial drain was extremely painful for a public company.

Through it all, he was regularly apologizing to his wife, whose medical treatment had succeeded, for how stressed he was, for missing events involving their son and daughter, and for focusing on nothing but the company. "This is all about survival," he explained. And focus meant a chance to survive.

Neal began sending signals to the industry that he was planning to carry on without Electrolux. He renamed the company Laundrylux to make a clean break from his father's management. He went to trade shows in Europe that Electrolux attended and ostentatiously visited the booths of their competitors, looking at other laundry product lines to replace Electrolux. He plowed money into improving the company's offices and showroom, hired new salespeople, increased his advertising, and, most importantly, ramped up sales. "Though I had a terminated contract—*empty pockets*—I acted boldly and with confidence."

In the process of turning the company around while still battling for survival, Neal realized the advantage that an entrepreneur has in a conflict with a public company. As he told Electrolux's North American commercial laundry chief, who was angling to be in charge after Neal's business died: "Electrolux has more resources than I do; you've got more money, more factories, and more lawyers than I do. In fact, you have more of everything, except for one thing: I have more willpower than you." Neal realized that while he could run his business at break-even or lose money for an extended period after his contract expired, no corporate manager could lose money for long and keep his job. As tough as Neal was, however, he was also smart enough to give his opponent a pathway to a beneficial compromise. "I'd like to work with Electrolux," he told them, "but I don't have a contract. I will either be your worst nightmare in this market or your strongest advocate. It's your choice."

In 2009, less than a year before the seven-year window closed, Neal got a call from Electrolux's professional division headquarters in Pordenone, Italy, inviting him to see their new machines, which would be introduced the following year when he no longer had a contract with Electrolux. Neal had already seen the new models months earlier, and his hosts knew that. He flew to Italy, dutifully marveled at the products, and then went to a prearranged dinner. "Instead of all those product people, the entire top brass shows up, about twelve Electrolux people and me." Neal knew all of them, so the conversation was pleasant, the food delicious, and the wine excellent. During a lull in the conversation after the main course, Neal piped up: "So, gentlemen, is there anything else on your mind?" The senior executive at the table cleared his throat and responded: "We want to know if we can make a deal with you." Electrolux asked Neal to terminate the trademark litigation and negotiate a new long-term distribution contract.

"My heart leapt higher than any high jumper in Olympic history," Neal recalls. "I had been playing poker without even holding a pair, but acting with the confidence of a card shark holding a straight flush. My intense focus and persistence had brought me back from near business extinction to life." Neal had inflicted enough pain that Electrolux wanted it to cease. But he had also shown them a path to a brighter future by increasing sales and marketing. "That's all they and I really wanted," says Neal. "I give them credit for reaching the right decision under very difficult circumstances."

Now that his seven-year battle to retain a lucrative product line was over, he had to immediately shift his attention to working out an equitable deal with his older brother to gain complete control of the family business while also correcting the "massive number of mistakes" his father had made in estate planning and dealing with the IRS on the back taxes the company owed. "It seemed to be an unending stream of things I had to deal with, but I dealt with it all." It took three more years to settle amicably with his brother and resolve all financial matters. Instead of taking a victory lap, Neal refocused his energies on driving Laundrylux's growth, including major investments in sales staff, training, and distributor relations, as well as novel cloud-based software solutions for financing equipment and contract manufacturing in China, which restored the company's reputation as an innovative and profitable leader in its industry. Laundrylux more than doubled revenues and quadrupled profits, and it continues to grow faster than its competitors.

It's an amazing story. And Goleman's analysis of having a triple focus helped me make sense of Neal's achievement. First, he knew he had the talent and deep knowledge of the commercial laundry business and the sheer drive needed to save the family company (i.e., inner focus). Second, he was able to calm his creditors, restore the morale of his employees and distributors, and detect the weaknesses of his opponents (i.e., other focus). Finally, he recognized the needs of a new generation of computer-literate customers (i.e., outer focus).

But how does a business owner in the midst of an existential threat turn innovative? Where does that creativity come from? Goleman offers a partial explanation, noting that business schools today teach the difference between strategies that are *exploitive* (improving the existing business model or technology) and *explorative* (finding a new way to do business). "A new strategy," he writes, "means reorienting from what's now business as usual to a fresh focus." Research shows that companies that can manage being both exploitive and explorative soar. But how do you juggle sticking to what's worked with searching for a more creative way to expand your company? I found one possible answer in some research published in the academic journal *Frontiers of Neuroscience* in 2014. Brain scans of managers and entrepreneurs involved in explorative tasks found that entrepreneurs were more likely to think creatively, using the right, creative side of the prefrontal cortex of their brains as well as the rational left side. Managers primarily stuck with rational left-brained thinking.[4]

Fascinating stuff, for entrepreneurs anyway: we actually appear to think *differently*. And yes, this multiple focus can be learned. According to Goleman, neuroscientists have found that the ability to focus attention "works much like a muscle—use it poorly and it can wither; work it well and it grows."

Notes

1. UBS and PwC, "UBS/PwC 2015 Billionaire Report" (2015), http://www.pwchk .com/en/migration/pdf/billionaire-report-2015.pdf.
2. Daniel Goleman, *Focus: The Hidden Driver of Excellence* (New York: HarperCollins, 2013).
3. Neal Milch, interview (June 10, 2016).
4. Daniella Laureiro-Martínez, Nicola Canessa, Stefano Brusoni, Maurizio Zollo, Todd Hare, Federica Alemanno, and Stefano F. Cappa, "Frontopolar Cortex and Decision-Making Efficiency: Comparing Brain Activity of Experts with Different Professional Backgrounds During an Exploration-Exploitation Task," *Frontiers in Human Neuroscience* (January 22, 2014). One of the authors, Maurizio Zollo, summarized the research in an MIT blog: http://mitsloanexperts.mit.edu/the-innovative-brain-maurizio-zollo/.

LESSON 21

Curiosity Fuels Creativity

Over the years, I came to understand that what keeps me going to Tiger 21 meetings—and attracts so many others to our organization—is a lifelong passion for learning. According to many of our chairs, the high curiosity quotient of members is what makes their jobs so rewarding and so much fun. "They are constant life learners and genuinely curious and enjoy the fellowship of other like-minded people," reports Chris Ryan, who chairs our groups in Dallas and Austin and is co-chair of our group in Puerto Rico. "When you get that unique combination of amazing people in a room, you can really create something significant."[1]

I leave almost every Tiger 21 meeting with a new shortlist of books I should read, which means that I end every year with a very long list of books I haven't had time to read. Is our membership brimming with scholars and intellectuals? Quite the contrary, though we do have our share of PhDs, MBAs, and JDs.

I'm sure you have academically successful friends and relatives who care only about their subject and have never shown any curiosity about yours, such as that company you've devoted your life to. Often the most curious among our members are those with the sketchiest educational backgrounds, who've developed a passion for self-education. A retired co-chairman of a major New York investment bank in one of my groups never went to college but knows as much about history and neurology as many specialists. And he has street smarts too. Managing hundreds of high-powered traders taught him to smell a rat from a mile away.

For many members, Tiger 21 meetings are the only time they can step away from the details of their business, family, and philanthropic concerns and nurture their curiosity among a group of equally curious peers. "I enjoy spending a day with twelve or so people from different backgrounds and experiences from what I deal with day to day," says one longtime member. "The meetings create a different kind of stimulation for my mind." And remember, these aren't just any 12 people. Every one of them has, on average, figured out some part of the business world, in some cases better than just about anyone else in the world.

Native curiosity is typically a key factor in how entrepreneurs are able to see potential businesses where no one else does. That curiosity engine is also what drives a business founder to come up with innovations to beat the competition or even become a billionaire. According to UBS and PwC's joint report on billionaires, "Curiosity is a core skill of the self-made billionaires we met . . . constantly driving them to look for unmet customer needs that create significant business opportunity."[2]

Curiosity has certainly pulled me in directions I would have never anticipated when I was dreaming of launching my own real estate business as a teenager. When I was in my twenties and focused on growing my first company, I had the opportunity to view some early solar research the Israelis were doing in the desert, and I became fascinated with the possibilities of wireless power. The prospect of an alternative energy source that would reduce America's dependence on oil came to occupy such a large corner of my imagination that a number of years later an idea popped into my head for a solar unit the size of a thick Frisbee that could power a light or a camera or perhaps open a gate. A few weeks later, I happened to get an invitation to visit a company in Florida that was pioneering solar outdoor lighting systems, and I couldn't resist investing in it.

Over the next 25 years, I continued funding that company because I believed solar-powered outdoor lighting for roads, pathways, and parking lots would eventually be cheaper than electric grid–tied lighting. Solar outdoor lighting is not the same as solar power or other alternative energy opportunities. The economics are not as related to the cost of electricity as you might think because the real savings are in the avoided costs associated with the installation. With solar outdoor lighting, you avoid all the costs of digging trenches and laying wires in them that connect back to the grid. And did I mention that the energy is free? After 25 years of supporting that company, I merged it into a larger company in an adjacent space, of which I am now chairman.

I will save my pitch for social entrepreneurship for the final section of this book (Lesson 39). Suffice it to say that my investments in solar power allow me to combine my career as a serial entrepreneur with my commitment to reducing America's (and the world's) dependence on fossil fuels, particularly coal, while battling the effects of climate change.

Tiger 21 was also the result of my curiosity. I'd long wondered whether there was an organization where a successful entrepreneur but rookie investor like myself could get objective advice from world-class investors who had already traveled the journey from entrepreneur to wealth preserver. There was none, so I pulled together a group consisting of some Wall Street pros and fellow entrepreneurs who had also sold their businesses to meet regularly.

I hear about the phenomenal effects of curiosity all the time. Once Neal Milch (Lesson 20) saved his family company from a fire sale and restored it to glory, he could have sat back and counted his money.[3] Instead, he began wondering how he could bring his company into the Internet Age. He had noticed a new cohort of people entering the business who didn't want to face the upfront capital costs of buying commercial laundry machines. Neal explored the possibility of charging them for using machines that his company supplied. The genius of the idea was to turn a commercial laundry into a utility in which you pay as you go, just as you do for using electricity or gas. "I invented this whole new concept of connecting laundry equipment to the cloud," he says, quite amazed that he had created a tech business.

By paying attention to what was happening outside his industry, Neal was able to conceive a whole new business model with the technology and algorithm that could not only track use but also monitor the machines and alert his company about the need for repairs. Neal put together a team that built the next big thing in the very old business of doing laundry—and the customers came.

Yes, entrepreneurs need an idea, they need passion, and they need self-confidence and grit to keep their businesses afloat. But to grow a company, to stay out in front of the competition, to catch the eye of a buyer, and certainly to start a second business or more as so many Tiger 21 entrepreneurs have done, you have to show some imagination in figuring out how to better serve your clients and create new customers and new products and even new product categories and business models. That's where curiosity can become an effective business tool for refocusing your growth strategy.

How do you leverage it? I recommend that you start by asking yourself some tough questions about your business, its future, and your customers: What do they need that you're not offering? How do you boost your business to the next level? Do you need to change your business model? Do you need to bring in someone to help you? As the legendary Silicon Valley entrepreneur Andy Grove titled his book, *Only the Paranoid Survive.* If you aren't always trying to find a better way to do business, chances are you are already falling behind and may never catch up.

Notes

1. Chris Ryan, interview (July 12, 2015).
2. UBS and PwC, "UBS/PwC 2015 Billionaire Report" (2015), http://www.pwchk .com/en/migration/pdf/billionaire-report-2015.pdf.
3. Neal Milch, interview (June 10, 2016).

Think Bigger

When you ask the entrepreneurs in Tiger 21 how they became so successful, typically they shrug and say, "I got lucky."[1] I got lucky too, but if you create great companies, you've got something more than just luck going for you. Getting a better answer for what separates great entrepreneurs from the rest of us is one of the reasons I wrote this book.

"They always want to do one more deal, open one more branch—to go one step higher," says Cal Simmons of Washington, DC. "Most people are content to be successful with just one step."

I often seek out Cal for advice because, as an entrepreneur who created two companies and sold them while simultaneously branching out as an investor, he has a unique perspective on wealth creation. In many ways, he's a classic entrepreneur, a self-made man from a middle-class background who had a paper route as a kid and was a good-enough tennis player to make spending money giving lessons. In college, he started a publishing company. The day he graduated, he started Washington Tennis Services, which took a management fee for scheduling lessons with tennis pros at indoor tennis centers. Three years later, with a stable of teaching pros working in 30 states, Cal sold the company. He was 25.

"Business was easy for me," he explains. After dabbling in real estate and publishing for a year, Cal figured that he could combine his urge to travel with his love of business by opening a travel agency. He rented space in a busy neighborhood. "Six months later, I was making money," he recalls, still with a sense of the wonder of it all.

One day, a friend and mentor stopped by the office and said, "Cal, I know a spot in Georgetown where you could open your second branch." Cal was pleased that the one he had opened was doing well, and frankly, that was the limit of his then-current ambitions. His friend was incredulous. "You could have ten of these," Cal recalls him saying. "Without that one sentence, I might have never moved off my path," he says. "But once I opened that second location, I was immediately thinking about a third and a fourth and a fifth." In an industry where agencies bought the same tickets from the same airlines and booked the same hotels, Cal had found a way to separate himself from his competition: "While others were satisfied with one business, I now wanted ten."

Within six years Cal had his 10 branches. "I became 'Cal Simmons, the travel guy.'" After 23 years he sold the business, but he missed being the travel guy, so he started an online site specializing in luxury travel, which had outstripped the 20-year value of his bricks-and-mortar operation when he sold it four years later.

By most measures, Cal has been a very successful entrepreneur and investor. By his own measure, not so much. "I think what separates the really successful people, the kind who become our members, is that they think bigger."

Cal has hit on what I now think is a key factor that often separates great entrepreneurs from everyone else. Unlike most business leaders who set a reasonable goal for their company and then proceed to get there step by step, great entrepreneurs set a horizon that could be 10 or 20 years in the future, which seems delusional to most of the people around them. Management gurus used to recommend such long-term targets—dubbed *BHAGs* for big, hairy, audacious goals—to inspire employees or give them a finish line.[2] Unlike even superstar CEOs who are inhibited from setting goals that are so big and hairy that they scare the board or stockholders, entrepreneurs are untethered. They own the show and are beholden only to their vision and imagination.

That's where the serious wealth lies, way out there on the far side of the possible: in visions of a world where there's a personal computer on every desk and in every home; where anyone can buy any book (or anything else) over the Internet; and where you can make all the information in the world accessible with a click. That's how big the founders of Microsoft, Amazon, and Google dared to think, and you can be sure that many of their family and friends thought they were nuts.

Now let me quickly assure my fellow entrepreneurs who may not be computer or programming geniuses that a multimillion-dollar outlier can also be as low-tech as a burger and fries—to be specific, Five Guys burgers and fries.

You've probably heard of Five Guys, or maybe even visited one of its franchises in the United States or Canada. What you may not know is that this company is one of the great American success stories of the twenty-first century. The Five Guys phenomenon was hatched in 1986 in the Virginia home of Jerry Murrell, who was a stock and bond seller at the time. Jerry's two oldest sons didn't want to go to college. In an unusual display of family solidarity, Jerry—and his second wife, Janie—offered to invest the boys' college tuition in a burgers and fries "to go" joint that was inspired by a stand in Ocean City, Maryland, that sold only french fries that were so delicious there was always a line outside its door.[3]

The Murrells called it Five Guys for Jerry and his four sons. Their primary mission was to focus on the quality of the food, which is why the interior design of the shops is simply red and white tiles. "We don't spend money on décor," Jerry has often explained. "But we'll go overboard on the food." That means lean beef, hand-formed burgers made to order, 17 possible toppings, and toasted buns baked fresh every morning. The Murrells tested 16 kinds of mayonnaise before choosing the winner.

The customers responded, voting Five Guys' burger number one in the DC metro area. The family perfected their system into the 1990s, when the Murrells had another son. By then, Jerry was thinking big—one for each of his sons.

His older sons, however, were already thinking even bigger. "My kids wanted to franchise from the start," he recalls.[4] Skeptical that a Virginia burger stand could compete with McDonald's and Burger King, banks wouldn't lend them the $300,000 or more required to expand into sit-down restaurants. Finally, in late 2002, with five restaurants in place in the DC metro area, Jerry agreed, "kicking and screaming," to franchises in Virginia and Maryland.[5] Over the next 18 months, Five Guys sold options for more than 300 franchises. Today there are more than 1,000 locations in the United States and Canada, with 1,500 more in development.

I'm not an investor in Five Guys, but Cal is, although he almost missed the boat. When the company began franchising, Cal was offered the franchises in one state—he passed. He was later offered another state, and he passed again. "When I came to my senses, most of the country was sold out," he confesses. He finally bought rights to open shops in two other states. "It's probably half my net worth right now," he says gratefully. But he is still second-guessing his career. "I see contemporaries of mine like Jerry who have built very large businesses. And I sometimes wonder if I had focused on just one thing, could I have built it much bigger?" Join the club, Cal.

If you'd like to stay out of our second-guessers club, take a break to reevaluate your dreams and your business plans by asking just one little question: *Should I be thinking bigger?*

Notes

1. Cal Simmons, interviews (December 2, 2012, and February 1–4, 2015).
2. BHAG seems to have been first coined by Jim Collins and Jerry Porras in *Built to Last: Successful Habits of Visionary Companies* (New York: HarperBusiness, 1994).
3. Liz Welch, "How I Did It: Jerry Murrell, Five Guys Burgers and Fries," *Inc.* (April 1, 2010).
4. Ibid.
5. Ibid.

Think Twice Before Investing with Friends and Family

Nothing is more important to an entrepreneur than capital. And nothing can bring as much embarrassment, resentment, and peril to relationships with people you love and respect than losing their money. For your first venture, things might be different because people tend to temper their expectations, but once you are already a successful entrepreneur and people invest with you because they think it's a sure thing, watch out. The risk to personal relationships is almost certainly not worth the potential pain and anguish.

For too much of my career, I was not disciplined enough to say no to friends and family who wanted to invest in my deals. Often, I felt the urge to *do them a favor*, but accepting money for an investment that you are responsible for can be a huge burden if it doesn't turn out well.

Too often, a successful entrepreneur takes the money because he wants to be a hero—not because it spells the difference between making the deal or losing it. This is a sure sign that your excitement has blinded you to the real risks.

It has taken me more than 30 years to learn this lesson. Enlightenment finally arrived in mid-2016 as I was getting ready to buy a portfolio of photographs that could be worth many, many times what I paid for it. It seemed like the kind of asymmetric opportunity that I like—where the upside is many times the downside—and I shared my excitement about the prospects with a very close friend who is also a serial entrepreneur.

Over the 30 years of our friendship, Andy and I have invested in a handful of each other's deals, but I am sure we both feel that we were never a part of the other's most profitable ventures, though it is not clear why that is. Nevertheless, I told Andy I was investing $1.5 million in an opportunity that I believed could be worth $5 million or $10 million (or more). Andy was intrigued: "Why don't you cut me in for 10 percent?" I told him I would consider it.

After I closed the deal, which was very nerve-racking, I concluded that my venture was more speculative than I had originally anticipated and that it might actually be worth *less* than $1.5 million, though that $5 to $10 million valuation was still a real possibility. (This could have also been the usual fear I experience on some of these wild rides.) For three weeks, I agonized over whether to take Andy's capital. Not only was the deal riskier than I had thought, but bringing him in would be more complicated because, with an outside partner, I would have had to set up a separate set of books to track costs. More important, instead of being able to share the progress or failure of the deal with one of my most trusted friends, I feared the possibility that I might feel the need to filter our conversations and worry even more about my mistakes. Would our relationship change in small or large ways if the deal didn't work out? I finally called him back and told him that I valued our friendship too much to risk it on a financial transaction that could add an unwanted layer of psychological drama.

But I was still not sure I was doing the right thing, so I did what I often do when I am facing a difficult decision: I posed the question to Tiger 21 members. The question hit an unexpected nerve. Ambivalence reigned. As one member put it, "I vacillate between thinking it's my obligation to share great opportunities with friends and family to thinking it's a horrible idea, as no good deed goes unpunished." Another noted, "I have seen it work, but I have also seen it wreck family relationships." A couple of other members pointed to relationships with friends and siblings that had been ruined. Their responses reopened a deep sadness I have long had about the loss of a long friendship over a failed business deal.

In follow-up interviews, two members confessed that they found it hard to avoid since they never could have been entrepreneurs without the capital they received from family members. "At the very beginning I had no choice," recalls Rob Fleischmann, a software engineer in our Boston group who started his first company soon after graduation. "I was a young kid with only sweat equity to offer. Who else will give you money but family and friends?"[1]

Robert Oringer also confessed straightaway that his ambivalence about investing with friends is tempered by the fact that he might never have achieved his ambition to be an entrepreneur without his father-in-law's help. Nevertheless, Oringer has become extremely cautious about promoting his new ventures to close friends, ever since he invited an old college pal with type 1 diabetes to invest $50,000 in a diabetes-related deal that went south. "It was the first time I had ever asked an old friend to invest," he recalls, "and it was a disaster. I thought of writing him a check for the money or investing in a future deal for his benefit."[2] His friend, a successful attorney, told him, "Stop, I'm a big boy." Oringer stopped apologizing, but he never did stop brooding. "That loss is always in the back of my mind," he says. "I still feel a debt."

Fleischmann went on to create a total of eight businesses specializing in Internet infrastructure, assisting major corporations such as AT&T, Time Warner, Comcast, British Telecom (BT), and Vodafone expand their online reach. He's out of the startup business now, and with that distance he says, "My recommendation is, as soon as you can, stop doing it. Rich people know about the risks; family and friends are investing because they love you."

Another member, Robert Kramer, shined a light on an important variable in deciding to bring someone you know into a deal: "I am more comfortable with friends than family," he noted. "That's probably because I apply the 'big boy rule,'" explaining that he will accept investments from friends "who are sophisticated and experienced such that they generally understand the risks."[3]

Oringer has developed an even stricter set of rules. When interviewed, he was in the process of vetting potential investors for a new company he was partnering in. "I'm making judgment calls," he explains, "based on two criteria: their value to the new company and the company's value to them." That means high-net-worth individuals who not only care passionately about the problem that this new company is setting out to solve—a burdensome disease that is now incurable—but who also understand that it's an extremely risky venture. "Each one is an agonizing process," says Oringer, well aware that some are bound to be miffed about being excluded. "But I'm looking for people able to take and shoulder a big risk, and not everyone can do that."

Everyone echoed that your investors must understand the risks. Typically, family and friends blindly follow a successful entrepreneur or general partner into the deal without understanding the associated risks and business landscape. They assume that, given an entrepreneur's track record, they'll make a profit, and they are shocked if an investment goes sour. That puts the entrepreneur or partner in an unfair position, worrying about making up their losses at precisely the time he or she, as the lead investor, has probably suffered higher losses than anyone.

If you can't resist bringing in friends and family, make sure they are well aware of the risks and can afford them. Eric Silverman has "hundreds of investors" in his current business, "a hundred of them personal friends," and he makes sure that he is completely transparent with them.[4] It was a lesson he learned from investing in a friend's business. Over the course of three years, "I discovered undisclosed lawsuits, incompetent employees, fraudulent deals, and even some good old-fashioned bribes. What I learned most is that there is no substitute for truly understanding and measuring risks up-front." It was Eric's biggest financial loss, and it taught him an indelible lesson. "I must understand that when friends trust me with their investments, they expect a level of care that exceeds other investments that they are making," he says. "It doesn't ensure success, but it keeps me focused on being truthful."

It is comforting to learn that so many of my fellow entrepreneurs seem to agree that, for good and decent people, there is nothing more painful than losing the money of friends and family. Nevertheless, as reluctant as I am to bring a friend into a deal just to get their check, I doubt that I will be able to stifle the urge altogether. Starting a new business is always exciting, but it can also be a lonely quest. During my career as an entrepreneur, I've taken comfort in the fact that I have some friends who respect my abilities enough that they are willing to invest in them, even though we might not be batting 1,000.

If you too can't resist bringing friends and family into a deal, the "big boy" qualification is a must. In fact, my "biggest boy" happens to be a woman, a dear friend who has participated in many of my deals, winners as well as losers. What I most appreciate is her endless enthusiasm and support and the way she accepts a loss without blame or rancor; it makes me want to be even more successful for her. And so it goes.

Err on the side of caution. As annoyed as friends and family might be at not benefiting from one of your successes, they will definitely be relieved when they learn that they missed out on your big loser. Let me give Robert Oringer the last word on this important topic: "Yes, you can invest with friends and family. But never do it without looking at it from every angle. If you're their only ticket to score big, run!"

Notes

1. Robert Fleischmann, interview (July 7, 2016).
2. Robert Oringer, interview (July 21, 2016).
3. Robert Kramer, interview (July 9, 2016).
4. Eric Silverman, interview (July 9, 2016).

LESSON 24

Don't Overvalue Your Company

The risk of embarrassment before family and friends has increased for ambitious young entrepreneurs, due to a new phenomenon that I've noticed in the world of startups. Not so long ago, the billion-dollar startup was so mythical that it was called a *unicorn*. Today, *Fortune* magazine keeps a running list of private companies topping $1 billion valuations, which numbered 174 the last time I looked, including the following American companies in the top 10: Uber, Snapchat, Pinterest, and SpaceX.[1]

The result is that young entrepreneurs tend to get way ahead of themselves in valuation, which risks confusing—and angering—investors. Here's the problem: It used to be that if I had nothing but a great idea for a company, I might be fortunate enough to find someone who would put up $500,000 (or less) for 50 percent equity. Seeing unicorns in their dreams, today's young tech entrepreneurs want valuations of $10 million—and often much, much more—just for the idea. Recently, an entrepreneur who believed he was going to conquer the world of energy asked me to invest capital in an idea that he wanted to value at $50 million. It is a big idea to be sure, but $50 million for a company that just six months before had one of the principals invest $150,000 for 33 percent—that seemed a bit off the mark!

In all fairness, one thing I have learned is that the world is not round, by which I mean that not everything is rational and sometimes the pieces don't easily fit together to solve a puzzle. It is possible that those two entrepreneurs will solve the world's energy crisis and make billions of dollars, but their over-confidence, and the overvaluation it promoted, was of deep concern. True, I had a bit of that myself when I was 25, but as I have commented elsewhere in this book, one of the advantages of grabbing onto mentors when they are available is that they can add a dose of humility and perspective that younger entrepreneurs are often lacking.

The recent inflation in first-round valuations has been startling, even for professional investors. Consider how the average valuation of Y Combinator's startups has changed over the past few years. Y Combinator is a prominent incubator that offers advice and seed capital to promising tech ideas. In 2015, the average valuation of Y Combinator's 500 startups was reportedly $6.4 million,[2] which I believe is up from roughly half that amount just a few years earlier. It's true that this is an exceptional set of startups; they have to jump through a lot of hoops to be one of the lucky 100 or so selected from thousands of applications every year. But if the Y Combinator team deems your idea good enough, they'll invest $120,000 in exchange for 7 percent of your company, and other investors are likely to follow. With such prominent alumni as Airbnb, Reddit, and Dropbox, venture capitalists keep an eye on the companies that Y Combinator selects.

When a kid thinks his company is worth $10 million and turns to friends and family for capital, they are not likely to question that valuation in any depth because, for amateurs, it seems like the outcome is binary. The business will either be a huge success or a write-off, and in either case the valuation isn't critical. They just want to be helpful to their brilliant nephew who graduated from Caltech or their best friend's daughter who graduated from Stanford with a master's degree in computer science. Let's say friends and family invest a total of $1 million. The company is launched and makes rapid progress. The young wizard goes out for the next round of capital, tapping friends and family again, this time for a total of $2 million. The company has done so well that its valuation is now $20 million. Mind you, it might not have sold a single thing—the product might not even be finished—but success is absolutely assured!

By then the company is really cooking, and the founder goes out for a third round of capital, maybe $3 million or more, and seeks a $30 million to $50 million valuation, but because the capital needs are growing, it is time to seek investment from professional venture capitalists or a private equity firm. The pros are actually impressed. "This is a great business," they say. "It's worth $10 million—maybe 15." This happens all the time. Professional investors employ well-tested models for assessing risks and almost always arrive at a lower valuation than the optimistic entrepreneur. Suddenly, the business founder is faced with the unpleasant task of reporting this down round to friends and family. Even if there are down-round protections that adjust early investors to a lower share price, it is still tough to give friends and family bad news that will undermine their confidence in the entrepreneur's judgment. They will ask: "After all the progress we have made, how can the company be worth what it was when we started? And how can it be worth half of what it was valued at in the last round when all we have done is improve the product and increase our prospects?" The answer is simple: The friends, family, *and* founder were clueless and naïve to begin with about the real value of the company because their main mission was to get the company launched, and they had no experience or capacity to really assess the risks inherent in the investment.

The bad news may impact investor relations, but the damage to employee morale may be even worse because the most recent hires with high-priced options will invariably start considering fleeing the company for a better opportunity. That might leave the business with the least talented employees who have fewer opportunities to go elsewhere.

The solution is simple, in my opinion: When you set out to round up some capital for your new company, you can dream of a unicorn but look for the funding that you actually need to launch your startup on more modest terms, to keep it growing, and to build the evidence that will prove that it's a potential big winner to professional investors. In the end, if the company is going to be a screaming success, there will be plenty of profits to go around.

Treating your investors with respect will build trust that can pay dividends for a lifetime. Being greedy will close doors to good people for a lifetime (although I am always shocked by how often investors who have been screwed go back for more). Yes, investors are aware that entrepreneurs are passionate about their ideas. But someone will be more likely to invest in your idea—and keep doing so in the future—if you show some humility and try to look at your venture from the point of view of someone risking money to help you turn it into not just a reality but one that delivers exciting returns.

Overvaluing your company is a rookie mistake that will not only risk your relationships with friends and family but will also raise questions among professional investors about the competence of the management team, which would be you.

Notes

1. "Unicorn List," *Fortune* (January 19, 2016).
2. Tess Townsend, "Dave McClure Braces for Startup Valuation Drop," *Inc.* (February 12, 2016).

Live *Below* Your Means

The parsimoniousness of even incredibly successful wealth creators used to leave me a bit dumbfounded until I realized how central the trait of frugality is to the psychology of the entrepreneur, rooted in their capacity for self-discipline. (You see this much less with second- and third-generation inheritors of wealth.)

A few years ago, I flew to Washington, DC, to check in with Tiger 21 chair Cal Simmons (Lesson 22). Cal was late. "Sorry," he said, as he hustled into the room. "I just can't stomach the $20 valet parking fee. I was driving around looking for an empty meter."

"Why?" I asked, wondering to myself whether he had any idea how valuable each of our time was.

"I grew up in a household where pennies were kept in a jar," he explained. "I'm not alone in the group in being this way. So many of us have worked so hard to make our money that we really don't like to spend it."[1]

Cal had reminded me of something that is easy to forget about Tiger 21 members. If you put forth the question, "Who in this room is middle class?" the majority of members would raise their hand. No one is looking for sympathy, but most our members are self-made men and women who, psychologically, remain rooted in poor, working-class, and middle-class backgrounds.

George Heisel (Lessons 2 and 5) comes by his frugality naturally. His father ran a family business and remained frugal to the day he sold it. George got nothing from the windfall, but he was hardly surprised. His father had always been particularly stingy with his son, whom he put to work at age 12, paying him a dollar an hour. "He didn't give me any free rides," recalls George. "And I see that with other members too. They didn't necessarily have childhoods of abundance."[2] I've seen it too. Many members (including me) began working as teenagers. Hungering for success, they quickly learned that to make money, you often need money—and the only way someone from a poor and even middle-class background could accumulate enough capital to start and grow a business was to save it.

"People don't realize the amount of cash a growing company needs," notes George. "I was really frugal," he recalls. "I kept my own salary to a minimum, and we rented a house. My wife regularly asked me when we were going to buy a house. She didn't want to live in a mansion, just her own home." George laughs at the memory. "But it worked out."

Even when some success arrives, business founders depend on their frugality to keep failure in the rearview mirror. "Many companies fail because they don't have enough cash on hand for that rainy day," George explains, recalling that when he was growing his company, "there were lots of rainy days."

The scariest one was in 2006 when Medicare came knocking on his door, requesting a pre-payment review of his company's insurance claims. At the time, it was easy for companies selling medical equipment to get accredited as Medicare service providers. But to reduce costs and ensure vendors are not profiting from fraud, the Centers for Medicare & Medicare Services (CMS) is authorized by law to ask providers with a high volume of claims to submit extensive documentation from a percentage of those claims—*before* CMS pays for the services rendered. The pre-payment review process could take months, creating cash flow problems for even the most scrupulous vendors. "If I hadn't been frugal, I wouldn't have been able to have survived that," says George. "Most companies don't."

Many entrepreneurs, however, end up delaying gratification for so long that even when they can afford to spend as much money as they want, they don't. It's a disturbing irony for many wealthy people. "I still agonize about it," says Cal, who admits that even when he and his family go on vacation, he insists on flying coach. "It drives my wife crazy, but it's important to me that my kids fly coach. My father would roll over in his grave if I bought my teenage daughter a first-class ticket." Over the years, he has worked out various strategies and tries to take multiple family vacations a year to make sure that his wife and kids get to enjoy the fruits of his decades of hard work. I wouldn't be surprised if a significant percentage of our members still fly coach, happily stay in large chain hotels, or drive their cars five years or more before they trade them in.

Psychologists have noticed the phenomenon, and I'm happy to say that we have provided researchers with access to our members. James Grubman, a psychologist who has worked closely with wealthy families for more than 25 years, has given presentations to our groups and at annual member conferences. He reports that surveys over the years have confirmed that "between 75 and 85 percent" of America's wealthiest people report having "achieved wealth after growing up in lesser economic circumstances, such as working- or middle-class life."[3] They are what Grubman and his colleagues have categorized as "immigrants to the land of wealth."

Like all immigrants, they have to learn to adapt to a new culture—in their case, as Grubman explains in his fascinating book *Strangers in Paradise: How Families Adapt to Wealth Across Generations*, "the unique culture of wealth, with its new customs and new responsibilities."[4] Above all, these new immigrants to the land of wealth are frequently haunted by the prospect of losing it all.

And like most immigrants, I would add, they arrive with valuable lessons learned on their journeys. Many entrepreneurs I know would argue that their frugality played as large a role in their success as their ideas or business skills, ensuring that they had the critical capital they needed at just the right moments to expand their businesses and fund investment ideas. Most would say that during their wealth-building years—through their twenties and thirties, and often forties and fifties—they consumed less than 50 percent of their income, either saving or reinvesting the balance in their businesses. They lived *below* their means and often wondered how friends with much less money could justify living more lavish lifestyles.

"A penny saved is a penny earned" is more than an old proverb—it's a smart business strategy. Another way of saying this is that most entrepreneurs who build success over extended periods of time would rather sleep well than eat well.

Notes

1. Cal Simmons, interviews (December 2, 2012, and February 1–4, 2015).
2. George Heisel, interview (July 14, 2015).
3. James Grubman, *Strangers in Paradise: How Families Adapt to Wealth Across Generations* (San Jose, CA: Family Wealth Consulting, 2013).
4. Ibid.

Make Failure a Key Part of Success, and Don't Let Success Blind You to Even Bigger Opportunities

Writing about my mentor David Fromer gave me an insight about entrepreneurship that had never occurred to me before: The best entrepreneurs see opportunities where others don't—and then seize them. That was David to a T.

I could not have written a job description that covered everything that David brought to our partnership. In fact, if someone had submitted a profile like that to me, I would have rejected it immediately. David's style and work habits did not square with my picture of what it took to be successful. I believed, for example, that the more successful you were, the harder you must be working. David preferred to spend a lot of time away from the office.

But David walked into my life and offered me the opportunity to work with him, and as young and green as I was—and as different from each other as we were—I was lucky enough to recognize that opportunity and seize it. Many of the stories I've told in this book reflect people's capacity to recognize opportunities. Whether it's in a real estate lecture, a group of failing restaurants, or an unexpected business proposal, entrepreneurs find potential in unexpected places. In fact, an opportunity to create a successful business can emerge even from a moment of failure, which is what happened to Frank Rodriguez.

In 1992, Frank was three years out of Harvard Law School, working as an associate for a firm in South Florida where he had grown up. A married couple who operated a local sandwich shop where he regularly had lunch asked him for advice about incorporating their business. Frank told them to stop by his office the next day. During that meeting, they asked how much the incorporation process would cost. Following the advice of a more senior member of his firm, Frank quoted them $850, the equivalent of $2,500 for the same service today. The sandwich-shop owners headed for the door. "Why are you leaving?" Frank asked. They stared him down: "We don't like being ripped off."

After the shock wore off, Frank realized that his lost clients were absolutely right—and they had also shined a spotlight on a widespread need among small business owners that a smart, young corporate lawyer might turn into a business. Frank left the firm to launch Corporate Creations to start providing incorporation services for small businesses at reasonable prices. Focusing on client satisfaction, he proceeded to grow his company into the third-largest provider of registered agent and compliance services nationwide for *Fortune* 1000, Forbes Global 2000, and private companies. With thousands of clients, Corporate Creations' revenues have won it a place among the top 500 Hispanic-owned businesses in the United States.

I know firsthand the immense satisfaction of turning an opportunity into a successful business. But the stories that still amaze me are of those entrepreneurs who have built companies by creating beloved products—and then scrap that business model, which is actually working, in favor of a better opportunity that will take their business in a new and even more profitable direction. Peter Lobel did just that with his company, Tribeca Oven, whose small-batch, freshly baked breads had been a popular staple for decades in New York's top restaurants and specialty food stores, such as the local landmark Zabar's.

What most New Yorkers didn't know was that the company behind the justly celebrated and locally produced artisanal breads was the brainchild of a Zimbabwean man. Peter had moved to New York at the end of 1980, just months after his country had won its independence from Great Britain after an eight-year period of guerrilla warfare and international isolation. With Zimbabwe's political and economic future in question, Peter, 28 at the time, decided not to wait around and headed to New York to test himself "in the mouth of the lion."[1]

In the early 1980s, New Yorkers were discovering the joys of handcrafted rustic breads from the wood ovens of artisanal bakers, and Peter saw an opportunity to create his version of the American dream. You might even say he was born for it.

In 1946, Peter's father and uncle started the first automated bakery in what was then known as Rhodesia, turning the name of Lobel—the family was originally from Bulgaria—into one of the nation's most popular brands of breads, cookies, and other baked goods. Armed with a recipe from his father, Peter opened Hot & Crusty, a small retail bakery on the Upper East Side. That recipe, Swiss Honey Health Loaf, was inspired by a bread Peter's father had eaten at a health clinic in Switzerland, and it became a signature item. Soon, the shop's baked goods became so popular that Peter began delivering them to local restaurants and specialty food stores. In 1988, Peter decided to focus on the wholesale side of the business, moving downtown to the Tribeca neighborhood and renaming his company Tribeca Oven. In 1997, he moved his baking operation to a larger space in Brooklyn, and relocated again in 2004 to an even larger facility in New Jersey.

By 2006, Tribeca Oven had 300 employees and was delivering its fresh loaves to upward of 400 regular customers in the New York metropolitan area. "And then one October morning in 2006," Peter recalls, "I pulled the plug and changed my entire business model." Tribeca Oven stopped delivering freshly baked bread. His customers couldn't believe it. "Zabar's, which had been selling our bread for 20 years," he recalls, "refused to be surprised and was willing to pick up its orders in New Jersey. It was a seismic shift to give up retail."

But the decision was in line with Peter's very simple core philosophy of business: "Put as much distance as possible between success and failure." To put failure out of sight, Peter decided he had to quit the very business that was Tribeca's claim to fame and embrace a revolutionary trend in bread baking.

In 1999, another pioneer in artisanal breads, Los Angeles' La Brea Bakery, began shipping its popular artisanal loaves to grocery chains around the country *parbaked.* This means they were 80 percent finished and then flash-frozen for delivery. Suddenly, big chains, restaurants, and cafés could offer the delicious loaves that had once been available only in small bakeries. All it took to finish a loaf was to pop it from the freezer into an in-store or at-home oven and, voilà, a freshly baked baguette. "You could produce the bread non-stop," explains Peter, who in 2005 began marketing his loaves parbaked, with unintended consequences. "The parbaking [side of the company] developed to the point where it was interfering with our fresh bread business." In the new business's favor was the likelihood of reducing 400 daily deliveries into 140 shipments, resulting in dramatically higher margins and profitability.

Peter hired a CEO and executive vice president to help him expand Tribeca Oven's wholesale parbaking business, which put their famous New York breads on the menus of restaurants, cafés, and food stores up and down the East Coast. In 2014, Peter sold Tribeca Oven to a large Texas-based company with baking facilities in the United States, Canada, and Europe. "The American dream was alive and well," he joked.

In my experience, the dreams of entrepreneurs, no matter their nationality, will come true if they develop a nose for opportunity. Like every other arena, the business world is subject to fashions in management techniques, leadership strategies, and business models. And they all have their place. But great entrepreneurs resist getting locked into any one paradigm. The only constant is staying open to new possibilities—and seizing them. As my partner David used to say, "The deal of a lifetime crosses your desk every week."

And I would add that if you don't make failures a part of your success, it is less likely you are taking the kind of risks that often are the key building blocks to creating significant entrepreneurial successes.

Note

1. Peter Lobel, interviews (August 3, 2015, and February 4, 2016).

Don't Keep Your Family in the Dark

A California wealth research firm followed more than 3,000 wealthy families over the 20-year period between 1975 and 1995. They found that 70 percent of the heirs were unable to pass their wealth on to the third generation.[1] Such evidence has nurtured the adage that keeps many members awake at night: "Shirtsleeves to shirtsleeves in three generations." This saying appears to be well known in many languages across the globe. In Japan the expression is "Rice paddies to rice paddies in three generations." A Scottish variant is "The father buys, the son builds, the grandchild sells, and his son begs." An Italian variation is apparently "from stables to stars to stables." There are many others, but the oldest reference I could find was from Lancashire, which is "clogs to clogs in three generations."[2]

It should be no surprise that in a period of time where unprecedented first-generation wealth has been created, where many holders of such wealth have no family experience maintaining it, that the entrepreneurs who have created such vast wealth in the upper reaches of the 1 percent do not have deeply imbedded thoughts about wealth preservation (and if they do, they are often unproven). In a society where so many peers are also first-generation wealth creators, it is hard to be fully confident of the likely multigenerational outcomes of policies and behavior that other similar first-generation wealth creators exhibit.

The main reason for this is not bad investment advice or high taxes. Rather, 60 percent of the families studied experienced "a breakdown in trust and communication" among family members—in other words, *squabbling over money.* In a quarter of those cases, families failed to prepare their kids for the wealth they would inherit.[3]

Two decades later, the Americans who have moved into the upper reaches of the 1 percent are generally no better at talking about money with their families. Often, they don't realize that their children's expectation of inherited wealth can alter their behavior and motivation. A 2012 study by U.S. Trust found that more than 50 percent of wealthy baby boomer parents had not fully disclosed their financial situation to their kids.[4] In 13 percent of the cases, the heirs didn't have a clue about how much the family was worth. In *Strangers in Paradise: How Wealthy Families Adapt to Wealth Across Generations,* which I recommend wholeheartedly, James Grubman discusses cases in which clients deliberately kept their kids in the dark about how much the family was worth.

No matter what career stage you have reached, I believe the evidence supports talking to your family about your business and financial condition. That said, I know a lot of very successful people who have refused to do so for any number of reasons. As frank and forthcoming as our members are about their businesses, investment, and even family concerns during meetings, in too many cases those communication skills seem to disappear around the family dinner table. "The number one problem I've found among Tiger 21 members is a failure to communicate with their families about their businesses and wealth," confirms Patricia Saputo,[5] who grew up in one of Canada's most successful entrepreneurial families and has spent the past 15 years meeting the challenges of preserving and creating wealth for multiple generations.

In the early 1950s, her grandparents, father, three uncles, and four aunts emigrated from Sicily to the Montreal area. They started a cheesemaking company, grew it successfully over the next three decades, and finally took the company public in 1997. Thanks to a series of strategic acquisitions, Saputo Inc. is now one of the world's top 10 dairy processors, the largest in Canada, and among America's top three cheesemakers. With operations also in Argentina and Australia, Saputo has some 12,500 employees and annual revenues of almost $11 billion.[6] In 1999, the company asked Patricia, a trained CPA and tax specialist working for a major accounting firm in Montreal, to join the board. That same year her father asked her to manage the investments for their immediate family, including her four sisters and later their families. She set up a family office with a clear mission: "I may not be an entrepreneur," she explains, "but my job is still to create wealth as well as preserve it."

Central to that process is making sure each generation is well informed about the family's financial situation and how it relates to their own dreams and ambitions. Since not every family member can (or wants to) be in the business, Patricia seeks to inspire young family members with a broader definition of creating wealth or capital. Her pitch can be summed up with the acronym FISH, which stands for *financial capital, intellectual capital, social capital,* and *human capital.* A Saputo who chooses to become a schoolteacher, for example, might not make much money, but they would have the pleasure of creating a great deal of intellectual, social, and human capital.

Running a family office requires communication. "The problem is that when you tell an entrepreneur to communicate, you typically have a type A decision maker who will take home his dictatorial style and deliver a lecture to his family," warns Tom Rogerson, a senior managing director and family wealth strategist at Wilmington Trust and a recognized pioneer in methods for assisting wealthy families meet the challenges of family governance.[7] "It's not just telling your wife and children how much money you have," he says, "it's about making sure that whatever the numbers are, they have the capacity to understand and handle them."

Rogerson speaks with authority. He is a fourth-generation scion of a legendary Boston banking fortune and also had to roll up his sleeves. "My great-grandfather made all the financial and investment decisions for the family, and everyone was happy with that because he did a good job. But when he died, the next generation, already in their late forties and into their fifties, had grown apart and didn't trust each other, mainly because they had never made any consequential decisions about money together."

The way to earn the trust of family members is through "interpersonal communication," the kind of serious and mission-driven give-and-take that, ironically, as Rogerson notes, talented entrepreneurs employ at the office every day to get the most out of their teams of diverse managers. While family vacations are great, you're not likely to discuss issues of consequence with your spouse and kids at the beach. According to Rogerson, "The research shows that families that succeed generation after generation institutionalize interpersonal communications between family members—in the form of family meetings." He advises clients to plan meetings around a series of educational components, beginning with testing for styles of communication and leadership. Then they can learn about how the family business operates and succeeds, becoming financially literate enough to understand the basics of the family's investments and the advantages (and disadvantages) of financial advisors and money managers. Finally, they must discuss the importance of tax and estate planning and philanthropy.

"There are no courses on this in college," notes Rogerson, adding that such purposeful meetings are also an opportunity for everyone to have the kind of "meaningful family experiences that reveal the values that you all care about most." This is a crucial point. In my experience, if you tell a business leader that he should share his core values with his family, he is likely to nod and begin jotting down a list to pass along to them. This list is likely to be quite different from the values that emerge from spending time discussing issues that affect the lives and futures of every member of the family, which can provide a reliable ethical benchmark for their entire lives. "The opposite of control is participation," notes Rogerson, "and allowing your children a voice in the family's future increases their buy-in."

I have yet to meet a family that has not benefited from the discipline of regular issue-driven meetings. One other tip from veterans of family meetings: If your kids go silent or surly every time you offer advice, maybe you're the problem and not them. We all have our own styles of communication, and some have been known to deafen the listener to even the wisest message. There are a lot of tests out there to gauge communication styles; make sure you choose one that will test how good you are at communicating *interpersonally*.

A related and final tip: You may want to launch your first family meeting with the help of a trained advisor or facilitator. If you kick off the meeting, everyone in the room may flash back to one of your deadly lectures and stop listening. So let a pro do the talking and sit back and enjoy participating in what is likely to be a transformative experience for you and your family. It will be worth it. Maybe not the first time, or the second, maybe only after years of investing the requisite time; but in the long run, your family will thank you for giving them the opportunity to learn how to deal with the wealth you have worked so hard to create.

Notes

1. Roy Williams and Vic Preisser, *Preparing Heirs: Five Steps to a Successful Transition of Family Wealth and Values* (San Francisco: Robert D. Reed Publishers, 2003).
2. Tom Nicholas, "Clogs to Clogs in Three Generations? Explaining Entrepreneurial Performance in Britain Since 1850," *Journal of Economic History* 59, no. 3 (September 1999).
3. Williams and Preisser, *Preparing Heirs*.
4. U.S. Trust, 2012 U.S. Trust Insights on Wealth and Worth, http://www.ustrust.com/Publish/Content/application/pdf/GWMOL/2012-UST-Insights-Wealth-and-Worth-Highlights-Brochure.pdf.
5. Patricia Saputo, interview (February 3, 2017).
6. Saputo, 2016 Annual Report, http://www.saputo.com/en/Investors/Shareholder-Reports/2016.
7. Tom Rogerson, interview (March 18, 2016).

Hire Your Kids with Care

A very successful entrepreneur I know once explained to me his philosophy about hiring family members: "I don't hire anyone I can't fire." It's a funny line, though I suspect his kids were not laughing.

In a few words, he highlighted the dilemma that entrepreneurs face when working with their family members. The fact is that most wealth creators achieved their success on merit, and to keep their growth and competitive edge, they had to create a merit-based organizational structure, pruning less productive employees along the way.

Then, enter the founder's son or daughter who may be great, but lineage was clearly the underlying factor in their hiring. That invariably raises the appearance, if not the reality, of a double standard. We all know of family-run businesses headed by second- and third-generation owners who don't really deserve to be at the helm. Some of them have no sense of their limitations at all. They expect longtime employees to give them unqualified respect and obedience, and they expect those employees to pretend that the boss has qualities that he or she simply doesn't. That's a recipe for disaster.

If you're committed to having your kids succeed you, how do you know if they're really up to the task? One insurance policy is to teach them to respect merit and superior talent; another is to find out whether they have the talents and skills to succeed in your business. Here's how three entrepreneurs I know managed to bring their kids into their companies successfully. One even discovered, to his amazement, that his son is a talented entrepreneur.

Frank McCrea had never discussed with his two children the possibility of their joining the company he launched 40 years ago in Toronto, the Professional Computer Consultants Group, which provides IT specialists to companies on a part-time, contract basis. Now known as Procom, Frank's company is one of North America's leading providers of staffing and management services for contract workforces, with 14 offices across Canada and the United States, managing more than 8,500 professionals.

To be fair, Frank faced more than the usual share of difficulties before he brought his children onboard. Tragically, his wife died of cancer in 2003. At that time, his daughter, Allison, was in college, studying business. His son, Kent, was in New York working for the investment arm of the Canadian Imperial Bank of Commerce (CIBC), CIBC World Markets.

Taking over the family business was never a topic of conversation between Frank and either Allison or Kent. "I wanted both my children to pursue their respective careers according to their individual interests," says Frank.[1] But when Frank turned 60, he raised the possibility of Kent joining Procom. His son was surprised. "I didn't realize that was an option," Kent said. "I figured that you were just going to sell the business."

Frank replied, "It wasn't an option until now. I wanted you to prove yourself, and you have done that. You have been in New York City for four years working as a research analyst in what appears to be a pressure cooker of a global investment bank, and you have done well. Both career paths are good options. Give it some thought."

Kent did, and he came back with some conditions for joining Procom, one of which was going back to school to get his MBA. In 2008, armed with his MBA, CFA, and two years of attending Procom's quarterly meetings, Kent joined the company's management team. His first challenge was a money-losing company that Frank had taken over from a client in exchange for money owed to Procom. "Kent figured out the technology, reconfigured the staff, identified what was worth keeping, and got rid of the rest," recalls Frank. "No one knew he was doing it." Then, at a management meeting, Kent reported that the project had gone from losses to projected profitability—within a year. "Everyone was impressed, including me," recalls Frank.

Allison's career took her down a different path. Following graduation with a degree in business in 2005, she worked in marketing for a few companies and also spent three years working for Procom, learning the staffing business inside and out, before she decided in 2010 that she also needed an MBA to advance in her career. Two years later, she was back in Toronto with a business degree from Oxford and a job with the global consulting firm Accenture, providing human resources consulting services in Canada and the United States. Not long after that, she went back to school to get a law degree. Allison was admitted to the Canadian Bar in the spring of 2016. She had found her calling.

Over the same period, Frank had had a number of changes in his own life. He had remarried, turned 65, and had become really serious about estate planning.

As a result, the McCreas engaged KPMG and scheduled family meetings to discuss issues. Allison took the lead, identifying thorny topics that had been overlooked but needed to be addressed. One consensus solution was drafting a shareholder agreement with a share structure in place that served each of the family members' interests and involved them all in the company's success.

Frank also made his case "that management by committee doesn't work—only one person can be the boss." Kent was asked to take on that responsibility. Allison had a career in law ahead of her and could help the company as an outside advisor, which she has done, "providing advice," says Frank, "that has proven to be invaluable." Once Allison became comfortable with her brother taking over Procom, Frank recalls, "That's when we became very close as a family."

Kent had successfully managed a branch for a number of years. He assumed the role of COO for Procom in 2015. By 2016, Frank had stepped away from day-to-day operations, confident that he had an experienced management team in charge, led by his son, with his daughter's oversight.

His advice to anyone considering bringing the next generation into the business is this: "Avoid the pressure of an expected role to give your children the opportunity to find their own path. However, once the decision is made as to their involvement, have a strategy in place to ease them into the existing management structure in a way that will allow them to prove that they're more than the boss's pride and joy. You want their self-confidence to be shaped by what they've accomplished themselves."

Ed Doherty, whom we first met in Lesson 5, would agree. Early on, he set specific ground rules for his kids about working for Doherty Enterprises, which now has more than 140 restaurants in New York, New Jersey, Georgia, and Florida. When his three children were in high school and college they worked at one of his Applebee's franchises in positions ranging from dishwasher to busboy to server to host. Continuing in the company, however, was not automatic. "After college, our children couldn't work for us for at least four years," explains Ed,[2] who wanted his kids to go into the business world to get a sense of their capabilities. It's a strategy that a number of business owners I know have adopted. My wife's family real estate business, for example, has a five-year rule.

Ed explains what else needed to happen before he would hire his kids. "They also had to sit down and have a conversation with me about why they wanted to come back and what value they could add to the company." Tim, his eldest, was the first to ask for a sit-down, after working four years in Dublin and in New York in the corporate lending department of the Allied Irish Bank. Ed told Tim he'd have to go through the Applebee's management training program, but he already had in mind what he thought was a win–win plan for both him and his son. Like many entrepreneurs, Ed was doing it all—from overall management to choosing every single restaurant location, which had been his specialty during his successful corporate career at Burger King and Marriott. He told his son he would teach him everything he knew about site selection.

Tim agreed to become the company's real estate manager. "He grew and proved himself," says Ed with the double pride of a father and teacher. After 13 years in the company, Tim now serves as vice president of development of all the company's new restaurants across all brands. He selects locations, negotiates leases, gets all the construction approvals and permits, and then oversees the actual construction or remodeling of the company's restaurants.

Ed's role as a mentor to Tim became a template for bringing his two daughters into the business. In 2005, Tim's younger sister Shannon had already spent four years as the marketing manager for the online division of a magazine publishing company based in Manhattan. Along the way, she assumed the responsibilities of two successive bosses, but she didn't receive the commensurate compensation. It was time for Shannon to ask her father for some career advice.

Ed immediately had an idea for how Shannon could fulfill his "must add value" rule. He tapped her to launch an Irish pub for people her age in a property he had under lease in a nearby shopping center where the company already had three other restaurants. Shannon was incredulous. "What do I know about starting a restaurant, especially an Irish pub?!" Ed already had a strategy in mind: He and Shannon would interview 10 designers and architects. She would pick the two she liked best, and after they made their presentations, they both would make the decision. Then they would repeat the process for the food and the staffing.

Shannon soon took the lead in dealing with the details and developing the brand. Since 2006, Doherty Enterprises has opened two Shannon Rose Irish Pubs. Shannon, who is married with three children, is now a vice president at Doherty Enterprises, leading a team to develop and market new restaurant concepts.

When Ed's youngest daughter, Kerry, lost her job recruiting MBA candidates for the Swiss financial giant UBS during the recession, Ed was ready for their sit-down too. He wanted to convert a restaurant location he had under lease in another shopping center into something unique in the area—"a sleek Soho/Tribeca-style wine bar and Italian tapas restaurant," something that didn't exist in New Jersey. "Your sister and I will mentor you along the way," Ed promised Kerry.

In 2012, Kerry launched Doherty Enterprises' second line of independent proprietary restaurant concepts in Clifton, New Jersey. Spuntino Wine Bar and Italian Tapas (*spuntino* is Italian for *snack*) offers 50 wines by the glass, and another 250 by the bottle, along with various small dishes, pizzas, meats, and cheeses. A second Spuntino opened on Long Island in 2015.

Though Ed's kids have given new meaning to the Doherty Enterprises name, Ed is still very much in charge. He works closely with his COO and chosen successor, who had a 25-year career at Wendy's and is not a member of the family. After Ed's COO takes over, could he be succeeded by another Doherty? "If they want it," says Ed, "they have to go for it."

That's a matter of ambition. What's harder to detect is whether you have another entrepreneur in your family. And you are not likely to know that unless you give your kids the opportunity to find out if they have the curiosity, drive, and appetite for risk they'll need, to say nothing of the necessary talent. And let's not forget one hugely important distinction. In the vast majority of cases where a child takes over a successful business, the suite of skills, temperament, and appetite for risk that allows an heir to grow an already-successful business is often quite different from the qualities the founder needed to form the business in the first place. In many of the best cases, the child is actually better suited to advancing the family enterprise, although they could never have conceived or started it.

Second-generation entrepreneurs seem to be the exception to the rule. But such exceptions will not emerge without the opportunity to blossom. Neal Milch, whom we met in Lesson 20, was able to prove his chops as an entrepreneur in the successful commercial laundry equipment business his father founded and ran with an iron hand. The Milch entrepreneurial genes proved equally strong in Neal's own son. As Neal was preparing to introduce a new business he had dreamed up, offering customers the alternative of operating on a pay-as-you-go basis using his company's commercial laundry equipment connected to the cloud, he asked himself, "How am I going to manage this startup technology venture while continuing to grow the existing business?"[3]

The answer arrived when his son Cody, who had spent the prior two years after college starting a film production company, came to him for some advice. Cody was enjoying the work, but his clients were not so happy with the results. "They want a $30,000 quality video but only want to pay $3,000," complained Cody, who was considering applying to film or business school.[4] Neal said he'd support him in whatever he decided, but before he did, he asked him to check out the "revolutionary new tech business" he was about to launch. Cody did, and he told his father, "Let's see if I can be helpful." Neal encouraged him to "make it your own business, run it any way you want." Cody dug in and was soon detecting problems, reexamining the business model, hiring people, and tweaking the algorithm to integrate the financial information from remote laundry room servers that the machines supplied into the company's enterprise resource planning system. Fascinated by the technology and opportunity, Cody never looked back. "He's on track to become president of Laundrylux before the age of thirty," says Neal, "because he's earning it with success."

Neal is as amazed as he is proud of the way his son has emerged not just as a hard-working manager but also as a creative entrepreneur and leader. "I wouldn't have discovered all this if I had kept him under my thumb with the attitude that *you don't know anything, and let me teach you*," says Neal, reflecting on his own much more contentious experience taking over from his father. He's also revealed the family's investments, assets, and net worth to Cody and his younger sister, Julia, and involved them in philanthropy and the operation of the family office.

Cody has fit in so well with the company's current leadership team that Neal is now speeding up his own succession planning. Meantime, Cody is gently prodding Julia, who works in sales at a leading technology company, to partner with him and senior management to lead the family company toward its centennial celebration in 2058. "I believe," says Neal, "that the trust, confidence, and respect I've shown my children is the best investment I have ever made."

Notes

1. Frank McCrea, interview (February 4, 2016).
2. Ed Doherty, interview (July 16, 2015).
3. Neal Milch, interview (June 10, 2016).
4. As told by Neal Milch.

Take a Lot of Vacations

When I was 25 years old and David Fromer agreed to partner with me, I was delirious with excitement. And then he presented me with one demand that was non-negotiable: If we were to be partners, I would have to understand that he was likely to disappear from the office many weeks during the year—or simply put, as often as he wanted.

I wouldn't have been more astonished if he had announced that he was a communist. I had grown up in a post–World War II culture where Americans at every level of the economy got an annual paid vacation of two weeks, maybe three for senior executives: my father had two or three weeks of vacation his entire career as an engineer and executive at NBC and RCA. At Goldman Sachs, we had two weeks of vacation. Even my father-in-law, who ran his own real estate company, seemed to take only two weeks of vacation, with a long weekend or two throughout the year. The idea of endless vacations seemed preposterous.

"I'm going to take a vacation whenever I see fit," David explained. "But you can contact me any time you want. I'm available 365 days a year." And he was. I never asked David where he developed his philosophy of vacations. Maybe it had something to do with his combat experience in World War II. David had been hit by shrapnel and passed out in a foxhole. When he woke up, he thought he was dead. From then on, he always felt like he was living on borrowed time, so he was determined to enjoy himself.

Not long ago I asked one of his sons-in-law if he had any idea where the idea of endless vacations came from. "If you asked David what the master-piece of his career was, the answer would be his family. It was the center of his life," he said. The long separations he'd endured when his family was in London and he was developing projects in Saudi Arabia made him all the more determined to carve out time for them.

David had lots of interests outside real estate—travel, art, and industrial design, for example. And maybe his insistence on disconnecting from the office had something to do with his idea that in an equal partnership neither partner should be looking over the other's shoulder. David was confident enough in his own contribution to our adventure to step aside and let me handle the day-to-day operations of the company. Of course, with hindsight, I probably minimized how critical his involvement with bankers, tenants, and employees was—and he took part in every major hire and strategic decision. But he was smart enough to fool me into thinking I had more control than I probably did.

The idea that your office could be wherever you were has had a profound effect on my own managing style, freeing me up to spend time on the other things in my life that I care about, such as family, philanthropy, political causes, and art. I spent four years as the *Official Volunteer Photographer* for the Princeton men's lacrosse team, on which my son played. Attending almost every game and taking photographs was a rewarding opportunity, while processing the pictures and producing four books was an added pleasure. More recently, I've been able to take the time to learn about Japanese art and culture.

Over the years, I've also learned that as much fun—or frustrating—as it could be in the trenches, the ability to get away from day-to-day concerns frees an entrepreneur to focus on the bigger picture, to keep an eye out for other opportunities, and to let the great team you have put together do what you hired them to do. For many business founders, it's not an easy lesson to learn. Having built their companies by controlling every move and cent, they have difficulty accepting that their train can run as well (or better) without them.

Frank Rodriguez, whom we met in Lesson 26, started his company in 1993 and relentlessly worked to grow it for the next 12 years as founder and CEO. He kept long hours, often working on weekends, except for the "few weeks of vacation with my family, typical of most executives."[1] Then, in April 2005, he learned that his 38-year-old brother had died in a kayaking accident in Africa. Frank was shattered. Friends and colleagues at work advised him to take some time off to give himself a chance to grieve and heal.

Frank decided to take a one-year sabbatical, and as a disciplined entrepreneur, he made sure he had a plan. He focused on three areas. "I fed my mind by reading books, watching films, and having interesting conversations," he recalls. "I fed my body by exercising five days per week. And I fed my soul by helping others through volunteer work, such as mentoring high school students." At the end of the year, Frank returned to his company ready in body and spirit to retake control of the daily operations at his company.

He discovered that, in his absence, Corporate Creations had had its best year ever. While that might have been enough to disorient some business founders into a depression, Frank was healthy enough to realize that his company was succeeding because "the management team that I had put together had filled the space." During his sabbatical, he had thought about the things he wanted to do besides work. He and his wife established Corporate Creations Foundation, a nonprofit organization with the mission of improving educational opportunities and health care for children. He looked forward to traveling and spending more time with his wife and two sons.

On the business front, Frank was able to focus on what he enjoyed most about leading his own company: strategizing for the long term and developing the kind of leaders and staff he could continue to depend on. Both were goals he could achieve while spending most of his time away from the office. "I've achieved so much balance since 2006 by growing my leadership bench," he says. "Each year I've gotten less and less involved in the details." In 2014, with Corporate Creations continuing to grow "at 15 percent or more per year," he successfully transitioned to chairman at the ripe old age of 50.

These days I also spend a lot of time away from the office. My guess is I am on 30 trips each year, and many are for multiple business reasons with a good number of vacations mixed in. For better or worse, I am taking endless vacations while being on call 24/7/365. Thanks to the magic of smartphones and the Internet, I'm in constant contact with my various partners and teams. Yes, smartphones have become a ball and chain, making it impossible to disconnect from office minutiae. But they have also liberated entrepreneurs and executives like me to be where we want while remaining able to be as connected as we feel we need to be.

There are lots of possible ways to lead one's life, but the unusual level of creativity that distinguishes the talented entrepreneur does not arise in nonstop meetings and deal making. To stimulate creativity, you need to find ways to let your mind roam free. No matter what your career stage, it's never too late to seek a better balance in your life. Get away from the office regularly. Give yourself some time to recharge your batteries and to think. It will be a win-win-win: for your team, for your family, and for you.

Note

1. Frank Rodriguez, interviews (August 14, 2015, and February 4, 2016).

STAGE 5

Protecting Your Wealth

For very successful entrepreneurs, the biggest challenge is often not making money but rather protecting the money they've made. Doing so requires them to adopt a new mindset and *not* think like an entrepreneur. This is especially so if they have sold their business and no longer have the regular earnings and distributions of a successful company to replace investment losses. The main reason why most entrepreneurs join Tiger 21 is to become a better investor, and our group leaders never cease to be amazed at how financially illiterate some of our new members can be. But at least they're trying to educate themselves. Most wish they'd gotten an earlier start.

This part of the book includes lessons that entrepreneurs should know about managing their investment assets, particularly after selling their businesses.

Entrepreneurial Skills Can Limit Investing Success

My 19 years in Tiger 21 has made one thing clear to me: entrepreneurs and investors are different kinds of people, inside and out. This is an insight that entrepreneurs can benefit from, particularly when they are contemplating selling a business. As David Russell, the self-described risk-aholic we met in Lesson 15, says about his fellow entrepreneurs: "Almost always, the way they got rich does not give them any skill set for being an investor. Basically, once they sell their business and have a lot of money, they are liquid and a danger to themselves."[1]

Similar sentiments are echoed in *Originals*, a recent book by the organizational psychologist Adam Grant. "The more successful people have been in the past, the worse they perform when they enter a new environment. They become overconfident, and they're less likely to seek critical feedback."[2]

While Grant was writing about airline and transportation executives, I think his observations generally apply to many successful entrepreneurs, especially those whose success is very deep and very narrow. It's hard to understand how limited your *great skills* are when they've brought you a really big success.

When David joined Tiger 21's first group in 1998, he was one of six entrepreneurs who had already sold their businesses. Group 1 soon added some equally successful investors so that we could get truly independent perspectives on managing our money from disinterested peers rather than self-interested professionals who were looking to sell us their products and services. Tiger 21's members who are professional investors—generally major real estate fund managers, owners or developers, or partners in investment firms or funds—never cease to be amazed at how little some of our Main Street entrepreneurs know about the fundamentals of investing.

The basic problem is that investors and entrepreneurs operate in ways that are, as David puts it, "antithetical." Successful entrepreneurs have generally built their fortunes by making big bets, often against the odds, on just one business—their own. Investors diversify their exposure across multiple assets; if any one of those investments fails, they are still in the game. A successful entrepreneur can pick up a lot of bad investment habits in the course of a long career without suffering irreparable harm so long as his company continues to earn income that replaces lost investment dollars. But once that business is sold, an entrepreneur can no longer turn to the company's cash flow to offset their losses. It's a big difference.

Barbara Roberts delved into this difficult transition in "Life After an Exit," a Columbia Business School white paper she wrote in late 2013 about the problems that entrepreneurs face after selling their companies.[3] A number of the wealth managers she interviewed noted that entrepreneurs posed a particular challenge as clients "because they could not give up control." As Barbara later elaborated to me, "Entrepreneurs ask lots of questions and need to thoroughly understand the investment before they step in. Wealth managers don't understand that entrepreneurs are not actually risk-takers, they're risk *controllers*."[4]

To me, that is more evidence that entrepreneurs and investors live on different planets. The only firewall between a small business owner and failure is being in control of day-to-day decision making—and anyone managing a great entrepreneur's money ought to understand that. As David Russell explains, when running a private business, "If something goes wrong, you can fix it. You can hire the right people, massage your customers, tighten your belt, expand when you have an opportunity. As an investor, you only have four decisions to make: what to buy, when to buy, what to sell, when to sell."

And if you are a passive investor or owner of a public stock, as most of us who've sold businesses are, then you find yourself to be the last to know about any problems your public companies might be facing, and you can rarely do anything to help when you find out because it is already too late and you don't own enough of the company to have any influence anyway. Mostly, you wait. For me, passive investing was like watching paint dry. And that is why so many entrepreneurs who become investors are way too anxious to *do something*—even if it's at their peril.

For example, the stock market has delivered average annual returns of 7 to 10 percent over decades. I have seen some studies, however, indicating that the average individual investor in public equities has earned only 3 to 5 percent. Why is that? Psychology. Many stock investors buy at the top and sell at the bottom, errors that keep them from even coming close to matching the historic averages.

Single-digit returns are not likely to generate much excitement for a veteran entrepreneur who has achieved great success building a business on his own. Real estate, where I made my money, is a world of big bets. Yes, you can take a drubbing, as many did in the 2008 bust. But for real estate entrepreneurs at the top of their game (and many kinds of private equity managers), they can double and triple their money in relatively short periods of time, even with conservative leverage, particularly in active markets like New York City. General partners of active real estate (and private equity) funds who might invest a mere 1 to 5 percent of the capital for 20 percent of the gains can do even better, earning 5 to 10 times their risked capital (and much more) in five years or less by leveraging OPM (i.e., other people's money).

Entrepreneurs and investors are also emotional opposites. Entrepreneurs tend to run on high levels of optimism; those who make a fortune are not likely to switch off their "Let's go for it!" mentality when they turn to passive investing after a sale. In contrast, successful investors tend to be skeptical, disciplined, dispassionate, and keen to manage risk. They make their living by culling through endless investment possibilities, saying "No!" to almost all of them. Reaching the top echelons of success in each area (being an entrepreneur versus an investor) depends on different disciplines, time frames, and ways of processing information.

Entrepreneurs set out to make things happen—to solve a problem, to get something started, to plant a seed. If that seed grows into something and then gets knocked down, they plant another. They fail as much or even more than they succeed, but when their successes outweigh their failures, it doesn't matter. Stifling all those entrepreneurial urges and habits to focus on preserving your wealth (*boring!*) is likely to be one of the biggest challenges an entrepreneur faces. I've experienced that crash from the adrenaline high of risk-taking firsthand. It feels a little like you're quitting the game, renouncing all possibilities, and coasting toward death. Shifting from aggressive and risky to smart and safe requires nothing less than a complete psychological makeover—and maybe some innovative compromises.

Rosser Newton from Dallas has built a successful merchant and investment bank focused on energy, which qualifies him to speak from experience about both entrepreneurs and investors. He has dealt with so many entrepreneur clients who can't resist taking risks that he's developed a strategy for handling them: "I encourage them to set aside a relatively small tranche of their portfolio for riskier deals. That way, they can satisfy that urge but still preserve their wealth."

In her white paper, Barbara Roberts notes that entrepreneurs eager to exert more control over their investments should consider private equity deals in their areas of expertise, so they can offer hands-on value to the businesses they invest in. A growing number of Tiger 21 members have been doing just that. After the 2008 financial crisis, just 10 percent of all members' portfolios were allocated to private equity investments, but by 2016 that number had more than doubled to 23 percent. That was also the first year that the allocation to private equity topped the allocation to public equities, which was 22 percent. That might seem like a small difference, but when we started tracking member allocations, public equity was almost two and a half times the allocation of private equity, so this is what the geologists would call a tectonic shift. Examples I like to cite are a printer who sells his company, taking a small portion of his proceeds and investing in a digital publishing company, or a successful taxi fleet owner investing in Uber.

Personally, I have come to terms with the fact that the traits that helped me become a serial entrepreneur—eager to risk my capital on exciting new opportunities—are obstacles to my becoming a world-class investor. I don't have the detachment that an investor needs. I would be constitutionally unable to jettison every one of my investments when the time is right (when is that, anyway?) without feeling a real sense of loss. I simply love the deals I get the most involved with too much—real businesses built on real ideas that employ real people and solve real problems.

Nonetheless, thanks to all those Portfolio Defenses, I have matured as an investor. I now concede that I will have to accept more modest returns in the passive portion of my portfolio to protect my wealth. My salvation is that the entrepreneur in me is still active in deals and new companies, and some of them are showing great promise for the future.

Unfortunately, we humans seem to have difficulty learning from others' mistakes. If you're a lifelong entrepreneur who had most of your capital tied up in a business that you have recently sold, it will probably take a few losses before you wake up and seek that makeover. Let's hope those mistakes aren't epic but more like the car accident I recently had that left me shaken but unhurt. If you are looking for good advice, start with your peers who have been there before.

Notes

1. David Russell, interview (August 28, 2015).
2. Adam Grant, *Originals: How Non-Conformists Move the World* (New York: Penguin, 2016), 54.
3. Barbara B. Roberts, Murray B. Low, Barbara Reinhard, and Bill Woodson, "Life After an Exit: How Entrepreneurs Transition to the Next Stage," white paper, Eugene Lang Entrepreneurship Center at Columbia Business School and Credit Suisse, December 2013. (*Full disclosure: I was one of the entrepreneurs Barbara profiled in the paper.*)
4. Barbara Roberts, interviews (January 14 and August 5, 2015).

Get Financially Literate

Why wait until you're *liquid and dangerous?* As someone who once fit that description, I think I have standing to say that it's never too soon to get smart about managing your money. Begin your education *before* you sell your company, so you won't put your hard-earned wealth in jeopardy.

"You need an investment philosophy," says Charlie Garcia, the Tiger 21 chair from Florida we met in Lesson 18. Before a new member's first Portfolio Defense, Charlie asks them to prepare a written presentation of their investment philosophy to help the group get a sense of their goals. "Some actually write 'My investment philosophy' at the top of a blank page. They have none. It's really kind of stunning to meet these incredibly successful entrepreneurs who are financially illiterate when it comes to managing their money and protecting their family wealth, which has been created from the sale of a business they worked a lifetime to build."[1]

Few people are better equipped to help others become more financially literate than Charlie. He founded a hedge fund, traded commodities, led a global financial advisory firm, and practiced law. Charlie views himself as a value investor in the tradition of Warren Buffett.

The members of Charlie's Tiger 21 groups are divided into three categories. First, there are those who have had a *liquidity event*, meaning their primary business activity is managing their investment portfolio. Second, there are those who have sold a business, so they have liquidity, but they are also actively running another business. Finally, there are those who are not very liquid because they are "actively running a business but joined Tiger 21 to get smart before a large liquidity event happens." Charlie helps new members face the fact that, as brilliant as they might be as entrepreneurs, they are not likely to become the next Warren Buffett. Their focus should be to become, as Charlie puts it, "the CEO of their family office—with the primary goal of protecting and responsibly growing their wealth."

Understanding the difference between entrepreneurs and investors is the surest way for entrepreneurs to prepare responsibly for the sale of a business—and the wealth preservation that follows. The next step on the way to becoming the CEO of one's personal investment company is to begin educating oneself in the fundamentals of finance and investing. Charlie reports that it takes three or four years for his members to get up to speed on the risks and opportunities involved in 15 different asset classes including stocks, bonds, mutual funds, gold, commodities (oil, natural gas, and other tradable natural resources), real estate investment trusts, private equity, venture capital, alternative investments, and master limited partnerships (which combine the tax advantages of a limited partnership with the liquidity of a publicly traded company). "And a favorite subject," adds Charlie, "is how to earn 1 percent on your cash in this financial climate instead of zero."

Figuring out how to pass wealth on to the next generation efficiently and effectively and how to manage your philanthropies can take even longer. Keep in mind that these time frames are for pretty rare individuals who have already proven to be at the top of their game in a highly competitive world, so for most others the time frames are longer—or never.

To help fellow members become more financially literate, David wrote a 50-page pamphlet, "Investing over Your Lifetime," which he has updated with spouses and kids in mind. Here is a summary of David's advice. Before investing a cent:

- **Protect your credit score**. As an entrepreneur, you should already know how important this is for starting and expanding your business. The higher your rating, the less you'll pay banks for loans.
- **Buy a house**. In general, your first best investment is your home, even if you have to get a mortgage to do it. *Note: I have noticed another seismic shift going on with millennials, who are far less disposed to own assets (and build credit) than my baby boomer peers. Fewer homes, fewer cars, less stuff. In time, we will better understand how millennials will succeed as entrepreneurs; it will be interesting to see what emerges as their best investments.*
- **Have cash for a rainy day**. Everyone needs some savings to get through a crisis (e.g., a business problem, illness, other unexpected expenses, the loss of a job). This means at least three months' worth but not more than

two years. *Note: There is an interesting contrast on this score between active entrepreneurs, who plow their cash back into their businesses, and those who have sold their businesses and now live off their wealth. Our community of 500 members, most of whom already had their liquidity event, tend to keep about 12 percent of their assets in cash. Since they live on 2 to 3 percent of their assets a year, that 12 percent amounts to four to six years of living expenses, in cash, on hand.*

- **Buy insurance**. That includes getting major medical health insurance, liability insurance to protect all the assets you've accumulated from being wiped out with one lawsuit, and life insurance if you have a family or someone (or a charity) that you'd like to take care of when you die. (Lesson 36 covers life insurance in more detail.)

- **Get out of debt**. Yes, you can deduct some of your mortgage interest from your taxes, but you should try to pay off all your other debts (i.e., invest in yourself) before venturing into the markets. There is no sense in buying stocks if you're paying 15 percent plus on your credit card debt. And *never* get a loan to buy stocks (i.e., buying on margin). *Note: No doubt, active managers of real estate and private equity (and the funds that own them) are the best managers of debt on the planet. So if you have those skills and want to be actively managing such risk, that's one thing. But most of our members want to keep things simple and minimize risks after so many years of living on the edge. Obviously, the many recent years of low-interest rates have encouraged more debt, but for those who lived through the Carter years in the late 1970s with debt peaking at 21 percent—and those who think rates are likely to rise from here—staying out of debt provides peace of mind.*

- **Commit to an investment/savings discipline**. To take advantage of the miracle of compound interest, you have to invest a portion of your income regularly. Investing every month or quarter will smooth out the ill effects of market timing (e.g., buying too many shares when the market is up), thus giving you a better average price over time.

- **Select your asset classes.** For most people—and for beginners, to be sure—that means investing in stocks, bonds, and maybe real estate. Leave investing in commodities and foreign currencies to the pros.

I would like to add one more from my father-in-law:

- NEVER EVER, EVER PERSONALLY GUARANTEE ANYTHING. The temptation to do so comes along every once in a while, and rather than recounting endless war stories, I will leave it plain and simple.

At this point, most of you beginners might be thinking, "I need some help here." Welcome to an old and ongoing debate about the pros and cons of depending on professional money managers to help you allocate your investments and deal with the risks thereof. Do you favor managers, or should you bank on low-cost index funds, which offer exposure to a wide variety of companies and industries by tracking the components of an existing market index, such as the S&P 500?

Most Tiger 21 entrepreneurs who have built wealth outside an operating business (whether from accumulated profits or the eventual sale of the business), have grappled with this issue, eventually reading a shelf full of investing books in the process. You too should do some reading. I'd advise sticking with the classics, or books by people you respect. Benjamin Graham's *The Intelligent Investor*, which had such an influence on Warren Buffett, is a must. Here's a short list of other books that seasoned entrepreneurs often recommend:

- I'm a big fan of *The Most Important Thing: Uncommon Sense for the Thoughtful Investor* (2011), by Howard Marks, a cofounder of Oaktree Capital Management. The book is based on the folksy and insightful memos to Oaktree clients that he wrote over the years.
- Burton Malkiel's *A Random Walk Down Wall Street*, first published in 1973 and still in print. Malkiel, who teaches economics at Princeton, argues that the past performance of a stock (or the market writ large) cannot predict its future movement, meaning stock prices move on a random path, up and down. He advises creating a balanced, diversified portfolio, preferably of low-cost index funds.
- *Stocks for the Long Run*, by the Wharton School's Jeremy Siegel, provides historical evidence that stocks have delivered the highest and most consistent returns over the *decades*—6.4 to 6.7 percent after adjusting for inflation.
- If you're eager for a brilliant takedown of the view that everyone will prosper if we just let the free market do its thing, you might consider *Irrational Exuberance* (2016), in which Robert Shiller makes a case that the market is neither rational nor efficient but rather driven by emotion, herd behavior, and outright speculation. One of the pioneers of "behavioral economics," Shiller, who teaches finance at Yale, shared the Nobel Prize in economics in 2013.
- Nassim Taleb, David Swenson, and Daniel Kahneman are favorite authors of intellectually curious entrepreneurs who are trying to make sense of the

bewildering world of investments. Their many books are as important as the individual ones I have named.

- Michael Lewis's *Moneyball* (2004) and, more recently, *The Undoing Project* (2016) were impossible to put down.
- Probably every one of Thomas Friedman's books over the last 20 years has been critical to understanding the political and economic landscape in which investment decisions are being made.

Charlie also points out that the Internet is an endless source of financial information. One popular educational resource is Investopedia.com, a well-written online encyclopedia of financial terms and strategies with educational videos on investing and personal finance. He also recommends the website SeekingAlpha.com, which features insights from a wide pool of ordinary investors and industry experts about markets, financial analysis, research, and investment ideas across a variety of asset classes. "I spend an hour on it every day," he says. There are also a number of very popular aggregator sites, which collect news from other sources in an effort to offer reliable, quick, and free information, research, charts, and advice to investors at every level of the game.

Nonetheless, I continue to remind myself that Warren Buffett is said to avoid having any terminals with up-to-date news in his office. He prefers to look over the horizon rather than the morning news. Buffett's mentor, Benjamin Graham, once likened the market to a voting machine in the short run and a weighing machine in the long run. To avoid falling into a herd mentality, try to avoid letting fads distract you from fundamentals. And although he avoids the endless distractions of every piece of breaking news, Warren Buffett apparently spends 80 percent of his day reading and thinking. His legendary partner, Charlie Munger, reads so much that he has been described as "a book with legs." One of the common denominators that the motivational speaker and writer Steve Siebold discovered after decades of interviewing wealthy people and writing his 2010 book, *How Rich People Think*, was that "they educate themselves to become more successful" by reading.

Frankly, it's a fool's errand to try to identify just two dozen or so books on the topic or even the 10 best sources of investment news or ideas. The books and media I referenced above probably represent 20 percent or less of the core library many members would recommend to someone just embarking on thoughtful investing.

If someone is trying to learn about investing, my advice is *read, read, read.* Investing is serious, challenging, and risky. One of the most common misperceptions among entrepreneurs who have had a liquidity event and are ready to start investing is that it will be easy. It's not. In fact, I would argue that it has been harder to manage wealth in the past 15 years than to create it, even though the popular perception is just the opposite.

Note

1. Charlie Garcia, interview (July 29, 2015).

LESSON 32

If You're Not a Professional Investor, Be a Passive One

My friend David Russell says that witnessing all the mistakes that entrepreneurs make when they become investors has convinced him that "people who become rich think they're not just smart, but wise, all knowing and all seeing."[1]

My take is that they are really and even uniquely knowledgeable, but only about the specific product, service, or industry they mastered to build their wealth. Often that deep knowledge is not particularly translatable to other sectors of the economy, much less the world of investing, which is very different from running a business with all its powers, information, and latitude.

I learned that lesson the hard way by losing a fair amount of money. The upside was that it inspired me to found an organization to help successful wealth creators grapple with the challenges of wealth preservation. The Portfolio Defense typically pours a bucket of cold water on any illusions newly minted investors might have of equaling the success they enjoyed as entrepreneurs. To put things in context, most members have typically generated compounded annual returns in the 15 to 30 percent range over sustained periods, maybe even decades (Warren Buffett delivered 18 percent returns over 47 years) to generate the kind of wealth that qualifies them for membership in our organization. Yet as prudent investors, it is hard to sustain 5 percent returns in the current low-interest-rate environment.

The message we hear from our veteran investors is that the main economic mission of successful entrepreneurs is to protect their wealth, and it takes years of experience to learn to gauge when risks are appropriate to various levels of expected returns.

That entrepreneurs are likely to be overconfident about their investing capacities no longer surprises me: overconfidence is what made them wealthy, but as investors they will have to tamp it down. Not surprisingly, two recent studies of the mindsets of thousands of investors and asset managers (retail as well as institutional)—in 60 countries—revealed that they too are inclined to overestimate their abilities to beat the market. In a 2012 survey, the State Street Center for Applied Research asked investors to rate their financial expertise. "Nearly two-thirds of individual investors rated their current level of financial sophistication as advanced," the State Street researchers reported.[2] Finding this result "overly optimistic," they did a follow-up study two years later in which they gave participants a financial literacy test. "The average score was a barely passing grade."[3] This reminds me of my father's maxim that "most people are stupider than the average."

State Street also found that portfolio managers tended to have an unconscious bias in favor of their own brilliance. "Without realizing it, they credit *themselves* for their successes, but blame *external factors* for their failures," such as market conditions, the expectations of clients, and the management of the funds they invested in. Yes, you will find that some active managers can beat market indices (such as the S&P 500), even over long periods of time and even when adjusted for risk or leverage. But the evidence also shows that past glory is no guarantee of equally high returns in the future. A 2014 scorecard of 715 American mutual funds that ranked in the top 25 percent in 2010 revealed that only two (out of 715!) of the funds posted top-quartile results through that four-year period.[4]

Even the preferred safe haven of high-net-worth individuals and institutional investors, the fabled hedge fund, invented to protect investors against market declines (for combined fees that generally include 2 percent of the assets under management, annually, and 20 percent of the returns), is losing its shine.

While a number of hedge funds boasted strong returns in the first half of 2015, between collapsing oil prices, a surprise intervention from China's central bank, and low interest rates, even star hedge fund managers were struggling by the end of the year. Billionaire hedge fund manager William Ackman's Pershing Capital was down 19.5 percent in 2015 and suffered additional losses through November 2016, losing all of 2014's 40 percent gain. Greenlight Capital was down 20 percent, and Glenview Capital was down

17 percent. Even John A. Paulson, the hedge fund manager who made upward of $3 billion shorting the 2007 subprime housing bubble, reportedly lost money in three funds. Three major investment firms—Bain Capital, Fortress Investment Group, and BlackRock—shut down significant hedge funds.[5] By mid-2016, the *Financial Times* was reporting that the hedge fund industry had lost $15 billion in assets in the first quarter, "as investors revolted against high fees and poor performance."[6]

Ordinary investors were also voting with their feet against the poor performance of professional managers, shifting $21.7 billion in the month of June 2016 alone from actively managed stock-picking funds to low-cost funds tracking market indices, the largest monthly outflow since October 2008.

And that's where you should be too if you don't consider yourself a professional investor (and perhaps even if you do). The evidence that picking individual stocks or putting your money into actively managed mutual funds is unlikely to help you beat the market has been compelling ever since Vanguard created the first index fund that tracked the S&P 500 in 1975.

Every few years, the financial media publishes an article on yet another study confirming that active investors across the board—whether individuals, mutual funds, or hedge funds—fail to beat the risk-adjusted benchmark indices. Larry Swedroe, a veteran financial advisor and writer, has called actively managed investment accounts "a loser's game."[7] In his books and articles, Swedroe outspokenly advocates *passive investing* strategies, such as creating a portfolio of assets in specific classes (stocks, bonds, REITs) by purchasing passive vehicles containing those assets (e.g., index funds or exchange-traded funds), which have limited turnover, low management fees, and minimal tax liabilities. Swedroe recently pointed to a Morningstar report that showed that over a 15-year period ending in 2014, the domestic and international passive funds of Dimensional Fund Advisors (which have historically offered what some would consider a *modified index fund*) outperformed 80 percent of the actively managed domestic and international funds that existed over that same time frame. In 2015, Vanguard's 500 Index Fund outperformed 77 percent of actively managed funds. Morningstar has also revealed that in the 10-year period ending in 2015, only 20 percent of active managers outperformed the Vanguard 500.[8]

Amazingly, millions of investors continue to bank on their ability to pick stocks or hire the right managers to do it for them. Even without including their fees, those managers rarely beat the indexes. But when you factor in their fees, fewer than five percent of them beat the averages on a sustained basis, and some studies indicate that the percentage is less than even that.

As a passive investor, you not only bypass those high fees, but you also don't have to keep one eye on your portfolio (or smartphone) all day, every day for the rest of your life. Keep in mind that even if you never call your broker to buy or sell something, the managers of your active funds might be trading like mad, which makes you a very active investor too.

Being a passive investor, however, doesn't mean just choosing the investment vehicles to fill your portfolio and then going fishing. Even when using passive vehicles, you must pay attention to what's happening to your investments—and to events in the world and the global economy that might affect them, up or down. Over longer periods of time, target allocations may shift as the investor ages or fundamental shifts in the financial world emerge.

The point is, it's really hard to be a successful investor, and talent as an entrepreneur just isn't all that translatable. Setting lower expectations is the first way to get serious about preserving your wealth.

The case for passive investing is so strong that even Warren Buffett, whose alpha credentials are indisputable—a 19.7 percent annualized return from 1965 to 2012—recommends that it's the way most investors should go. In his 2014 annual letter to his investors, Buffett revealed what he was recommending that his survivors do after his death with their share of the more than $60 billion he is reportedly worth: "Put 10% of the cash in short-term government bonds and 90% in a very low-cost S&P 500 index fund. (I suggest Vanguard's.) I believe the trust's long-term results from this policy will be superior to those attained by most investors—whether pension funds, institutions, or individuals—who employ high-fee managers."[9]

Notes

1. David Russell, interview (August 28, 2015).
2. "The Influential Investor: How Investor Behavior Is Driving Performance," State Street Center for Applied Research Study (2012).
3. Gary Belsky, "Why We Think We're Better Investors Than We Are," *New York Times* (March 25, 2016).
4. S&P Dow Jones Indices, "Does Past Performance Matter: The Persistence Scorecard," McGraw Hill Financial, http://www.spindices.com/documents/spiva/persistence-scorecard-june-2014.pdf.
5. "Hedge Funds Struggle with Steep Losses and High Expectations," *New York Times DealBook* (December 28, 2015).
6. Lindsay Fortado and Mary Childs, "Weather-Tracker Offers Rare Ray of Hedge Fund Sunshine," *Financial Times* (June 12, 2016).
7. Larry Swedroe, "Avoid the Loser's Game," ETF.com (February 27, 2015).
8. Ibid.
9. Warren Buffett, 2013 annual letter to investors (March 3, 2014).

LESSON 33

Diversify Prudently

One of the most valuable lessons I've learned over the years is that diversified portfolios of investments have the magic power to allow two people at opposite ends of a trade to both be successful investors, in spite of the fact that one believes the price of a particular asset is going up and the other has reason to believe it's going down.

Consider my friend David Russell and me, for example. Our takes on oil could not be more different. As I write this in 2017, I think the bloom is off oil. I don't only mean that some oil companies are going bankrupt tomorrow because of low prices. I also think that fossil fuel pollution, which is accelerating climate change, has put the future of the market itself into question. The year 2016 was the hottest year on record by a wide margin. Trump's election may change the dynamics of oil prices in the short term, but climate change will determine the long term. I believe if we want to survive as a species, and lead anything like what we currently consider normal, civilized lives, we must put an end to fossil fuel use soon.

In the short term, Middle Eastern countries need to generate revenues to fund social programs to combat unrest, which forces them to increase their outputs. Meanwhile, thanks to the fracking revolution here in the United States, we now have the world's largest oil reserves—and have replaced OPEC as the world's largest oil producer. Foreign oil producers have lost their pricing power. With fracking, whether you like it or not, the United States can ramp up production in a heartbeat instead of the two to four years it might have taken in the past. Add the impressive growth in renewable energy—solar and wind are growing faster than expected—and no matter what your views are about the environment, oil's long-term prospects do not look good. (There are, of course, events that could alter this prospect, including a terrorist attack on major oil production facilities, more war in the Middle East, or an unlikely alignment of producers to radically curtail supply.) Politicians can make hollow promises about a return to coal power, but unless someone wants to throw away money for social purposes, coal is simply no longer economic. I believe coal's demise is a harbinger of the future of oil, though its decline will be slower because of its critical role for powering transportation assets around the globe. No doubt the revolution in electric cars, and soon to be electric trucks, that Tesla began will be growing dramatically in the coming years with many more viable producers of electric cars and trucks coming to market.

That's my analysis, which, I will quickly add, not all Tiger 21's man-made agree with (to say the very least). We have members who don't believe in climate change, or who believe in global warming but don't believe it is man-made, and others who think the economic cost of limiting climate change is too high a price to pay in terms of human advancement. I respect those divergent views, though I wholeheartedly disagree with them. Such healthy and honest differences of opinion are what make our Tiger 21 meetings so interesting.

The broader point I am trying to share is that either of us could be right or wrong about our energy bets. But if we have prudently diversified portfolios, the one who loses out on his energy bets (whichever side of the bet he is on) has the potential to offset those losses with profits from other components of that diversified portfolio.

The goal of our confidential group meetings is to encourage the other members in the room (who are generally really smart people with deep and often divergent but relevant perspectives) to share lots of different opinions and options. We work through challenges together. Listening to all those views allows members to pick and choose the ideas or potential solutions that most resonate with their own understanding and act accordingly.

That said, virtually all of our members can see the benefits of diversification—a well-structured portfolio that balances the risks within it limits unwarranted exposure, and still is able to generate acceptable financial returns. But diversification is not so easy. In fact, it is one of the most difficult challenges entrepreneurs face when learning how to become competent investors, never mind successful ones. When running businesses, many entrepreneurs feel like they are riding a bronco. They either made it to the end of the ride and declared success, or they lost control and fell. In the vast majority of cases, entrepreneurs achieve great success by, among other things, focusing on nurturing and building a single opportunity or meeting a particular challenge (to the exclusion of all else), sometimes for decades.

Great investors, in contrast, are usually masters at puzzle building, ensuring that each component of their portfolio fits with all the rest. The long-term impact is profound. Winners overwhelm losers. Not every month or even year, but over the long term and more often than not. As I have noted, risk is in the eye of the beholder, a subjective quality that is underappreciated by inexperienced investors trying to value investments.

But risk is still risky.

What I've learned as an investor who is still in the game as an entrepreneur is to seek *prudent diversification* in my investment portfolio. Members are increasingly using the most efficient investments (like index funds) in markets that are the most efficient (like public equity markets). At the same time, they are increasingly focused on markets that are less efficient and where they are likely to have an edge, which is why real estate and private equity reached all-time highs by 2016 with 28 percent and 23 percent allocations, respectively. Energy markets may be quite efficient, so in that sense, a knowledge of oil, which is a globally traded commodity, probably doesn't give you as much of an edge as buying a piece of real estate where the experienced real estate investor can be armed with specific knowledge and skills.

Each investor has to come to an understanding of what prudent diversification is for him or her. A common regret among Tiger 21 members is that they didn't understand this concept better as they transitioned from being an entrepreneur, obsessively focused on a single opportunity, to a wealth preserver (after a sale) in need of a properly diversified and balanced portfolio of passive investments. But there's also the danger of getting too enamored with diversification, which is why our groups often discuss the need to avoid "di-*worse*-ification." At some point, diversifying becomes counterproductive. The returns that you can earn on a portfolio of 100 stocks can almost surely be duplicated with a smaller portfolio (a portfolio of fewer, larger bets), and when it is time to make a change, the portfolio with the smaller number of positions may be far easier to redirect. In fact, that more concentrated portfolio may actually outperform the 100-stock portfolio, and with less risk, but a passive index is likely to outperform both.

Clearly, there are many paths to success, and one person's ability to manage complexity may be different than another's. But according to hundreds of people I respect, an ideal portfolio should have in the range of 20 to 30 positions (or line items). As arbitrary as that number might seem, it is a significant data point for managing portfolios that touch on many different asset classes valued in the tens or hundreds of millions of dollars. Particularly for successful entrepreneurs who are grappling with the challenges of wealth preservation for the first time and trying to find some benchmarks to guide their approach. This also means that the average position will be in the 3 to 5 percent range, very helpful in gauging whether a position is too big or too small because if it is too small, even if it is successful those returns won't increase the total value of the portfolio in a noticeable way (they won't move the needle). It's hard to admit, but such small positions are all too often a distraction.

Yes, there are phenomenally successful investors who have scored on a far fewer number of investments and those who will claim their success rests on holding a greater number of positions, but that data point of 20 to 30 positions has percolated up over the years at Tiger 21 and remains an important guidepost for me.

Generally, the one category that is most commonly considered an outlier is venture capital (VC), where the risks are far higher and the rare successes even bigger. Many experienced VC investors feel you can't even be a respectable player in VC with less than 20 to 30 investments, although I commonly hear perspectives that set that number of investments at 50 (or more), and VC is just one asset allocation that might constitute 5 to 20 percent of a well-diversified investor's total portfolio.

LESSON 34

Spend Less

I founded Tiger 21 when equities were flying so high that reputable financial writers were forecasting a 40,000 Dow. But within two years, the party was over thanks to the dot-com crash and the struggle to understand the broader implications of 9/11. No sooner had the markets revived when the credit markets froze, giving us the 2007–2008 financial crisis and then the Great Recession, which spread pain throughout the economy, bottom to top. Wealthy Americans lost 20 to 30 percent of their net worth. Many lost far more. Many middle-class Americans took an even bigger step backward, and many have yet to recover.

Every time you think you've got a grasp of what's going on in the markets, the investment climate changes.

Knowing this is true, how can a mediocre investor protect his wealth? In the aftermath of the 2008 crisis, members of Tiger 21 embraced a variety of strategies. We reduced equity exposure, shortened the duration (the weighted average life) of fixed-income portfolios to protect against rising interest rates, raised cash levels, and even purchased some gold. Taking risk out of portfolios left many with materially more conservative investments, reducing income even more. A few chased higher yields in the beaten-down equities markets. Others dared to dip into principal to fund living expenses, hoping the downturn was temporary.

It wasn't temporary, of course, and the Federal Reserve Bank's effort to stimulate growth by cutting its interest rate to almost zero increased the challenge for anyone living off their investments.

Adjusting to a negative real interest rate environment changed the game for passive investors. Just to tread water, they have been forced to search for more yield, which has meant taking on more risk. Take a woman who owned a company that was earning $3 million per year. She sold it for more money than she ever dreamed of—let's say, $20 million, almost seven times earnings, a great price for many meat-and-potatoes companies. After she paid the taxman, she was left with $16 million in cash. If her conservative portfolio (constructed from the remaining proceeds of the sale) returns 3 percent annually, she actually is doing quite well in this treacherous environment. But the downside is she's got $480,000 in income to live on (including any taxes due on such income). That's still enough to remain in the 1 percent, but she was probably living on more when she was earning $3 million per year before the sale. And no matter how wealthy you are, a loss of 84 percent of your income can be emotionally devastating.

For virtually everyone, wealth by itself is useless. What's paramount about assets is their purchasing power: How much income they produce each year and what that money can buy, given the rate of inflation. To give you an idea of how voracious inflation can be: A 2015 $1,000 bill has the same purchasing power as $41.26 in 1914—a 96 percent decrease. If our entrepreneur had sold her company back in 1995, the purchasing power of that $16 million she had after taxes would have decreased 36 percent by 2015, according to the Consumer Price Index on Inflation.[1]

That means that anyone living off their savings will have to get a return on that capital that is greater than treasury returns, just to stand still. To fund their lifestyle, they will need even more earnings. As I write this, the Federal Reserve Bank claims that the inflation rate continues below its target rate of 2 percent and will do so for a while. But if you look at the basket of goods and services wealthy people consume, prices have moved dramatically higher in recent years—maybe at twice that 2 percent per annum benchmark.[2] And though residential real estate prices remain lower throughout the country, in some urban areas, like Manhattan, they have continued to skyrocket.

But let's accept the government estimate. In recent years, with short-term treasury rates effectively at zero, the real interest rate (i.e., adjusted for inflation) was negative 2 to 3 percent. In other words, keeping your money in the world's safest investment was *eroding* 2 to 3 percent of your wealth every year. Yikes!

Most successful entrepreneurs I know have told me that during their wealth-building years, typically from their twenties into their forties, they often consumed less than 50 percent of their net earnings, saving the rest or plowing it back into their business. To preserve their wealth during the years since the financial crisis, many have resorted to their default mode of frugality. Many Tiger 21 members have cut spending by 50 percent and are living on roughly 2 percent of their net worth. No one is offering any sympathy, nor should they, but the fact is that during the 70-year period since the end of World War II, nothing really approaching this has happened. Anyone living off their wealth today is in uncharted territory.

Spending is a serious concern. Consider an entertainer or athlete who isn't on the A-list. He makes a million dollars a year with an after-tax income of $600,000 and lives on every penny of it (and sometimes more). It's a great lifestyle, but barring injury or fickle fans, at the end of a successful 20-year career that celebrity will have no personal wealth to show for it: a $20 million career and broke! If that star had showed some discipline and lived on $500,000, and saved $100,000 each year, which grew at an average rate of 10 percent (to use a round number that is, admittedly, unrealistic in today's environment), he would be worth $6.3 million after 20 years. If he had lived on $400,000 a year, his savings would have doubled to $12.6 million.

The power of compounding plus a little discipline is extraordinary. Yes, it's hard to cut back on spending and save—except if you want to accumulate wealth and preserve it. What the financial crisis and our low-interest-rate economy have taught many of the wealthy people I know is that it can be easier to save a buck than make a buck. And the only way we can do that is to *spend less.*

Notes

1. Based on the United States Department of Labor, Bureau of Labor Statistics CPI Calculator, https://www.bls.gov/data/inflation_calculator.htm.
2. Federal Reserve, "Why Does the Federal Reserve Aim for 2 Percent Inflation Over Time?" FederalReserve.gov (January 26, 2015).

Don't Give Your Kids Anything—But Be Willing to Invest Everything in Them

I think I have your attention. And that's good because passing on wealth to your children is an extremely important issue that business founders should start thinking about sooner rather than later. It's certainly a concern that I've been grappling with as my children graduate from college.

And after sitting through 300 meetings over a span of 19 years, I can confidently say that the number one question on the minds of most of our members is: How do I support my children without spoiling them or destroying their ambition?

Many members are willing to admit that they might not have been as present for their children as they would have liked when their children were growing up, but now they're eager to do the right thing for their kids. What percentage of one's wealth should they leave them, they ask, and at what age? Should it be left equally to each child? Or is there another more equitable basis on which the wealth might be distributed?

Love comes in many forms, and among a good deal of wealthy people I know, that form of love is tough love. Some people I know will insist on leaving only a small portion of their wealth to their children or delaying the process until after their own deaths, when their children might already be middle-aged or older. The motivation is all too frequently to toughen up the kids by forcing them to be successful on their own because "they've already received so many advantages from me" or to give them the experience of making it on their own, "just like I did."

Of course, their kids cannot replicate the parent's experience because they've already grown up in a wealthy family, or at least one in which their parent's success likely far outstripped the levels of success the parent grew up with. Nor does this strategy take into account that leaving children less after raising them with more can be like pulling the rug out from under them at a critical time in their lives.

My own conclusion is that any will should generally treat children equally because an inheritance that is unequally shared has the potential to leave deep emotional scars in the children who inherit less, unless there are truly extenuating circumstances. I am not talking about children who have medical or developmental issues, which might require special trusts after a parent dies, though if the wealth is large enough, an equal share could still cover that kind of care. I am referring to situations such as the following:

- A family with a deep belief in public service creates a trust that provides additional support to children who work for the government, or as teachers, or in some other form of public service.
- A family with a farm that has been in the family for generations makes special accommodations to support those children who choose to keep it running.
- A family eager to encourage future generations to become members of the clergy provides additional financial support to those who choose that path.
- When one child goes bankrupt and is unable to fully provide for his or her own children while their other child is wildly successful, parents set up special trusts for the children of the struggling child.

There are endless variations of reasons to treat children equitably rather than equally, but I've learned that such approaches succeed (meaning that the children who receive less feel no less loved or appreciated) only if the parents make their case with clarity, well in advance, and base their decision on core values that have sustained the family over a long period of time.

We once did some role modeling in one of my groups featuring Betty, a 55-year old schoolteacher, and her 52-year-old sister, Susie, a successful investment banker, talking about their 49-year-old wastrel of a brother, Howard. The conversation begins when Susie the banker asks Betty the teacher if she has talked to their 90-year-old father about his will. Shocked, the teacher shoots back: "Susie, you are wealthy beyond belief. Were you expecting to get part of Pop's money too?" That ticks off Susie, who mounts her own offensive: "For 30 years, you've come home from a stress-free school at three every afternoon. You've never worked a Saturday or Sunday in your life. I don't remember you hopping on any red-eye flights to make an important morning meeting in Los Angeles, nor, frankly, have I ever heard that your job was at risk. I have earned every penny I have, and I don't know why you wouldn't think I was entitled to one-third of Pop's money, just like you. And I'll be damned if Howard is rewarded in any special way for being a lazy bum." And we are off and running . . . toward years of family strife, expensive lawsuits, and psychotherapy.

Then there are the complications of your children's lives after you've put the estate plan in place: the daughter with the big job on Wall Street at the time you drafted the will loses her job during the recession following your death; your son might have more children to educate than your daughter; one of your children or grandchildren could get ill or disabled. What seems fair now may not be truly equitable later.

Many members have set up trusts for the benefit of their children that will last well into the children's forties, fifties, or even longer. The downside is that the children will spend much of their adult lives lobbying or negotiating with third parties (some might say "as supplicants") about many different aspects of what is fundamentally their own wealth. I know I would resent that. Why would I expect my kids not to?

A relative has come up with an alternative approach that got me thinking: He intends to leave as many assets as possible directly to his children (rather than through trusts for the benefit of his children), who, luckily, are already in their late twenties and giving him a pretty clear sense of their trajectories in life. His objective is to empower his children to manage those assets responsibly as owners rather than becoming dependent on advisors and trustees.

This strategy is not without its risks. Direct ownership may subject those assets to be deemed common property in a divorce (potentially protected by a prenuptial agreement, bringing its own set of issues), or put them at risk in a bankruptcy or lawsuit of one type or another (although those assets could be placed in trusts controlled in whole or in part by the beneficiaries themselves). Nevertheless, it has the appeal of sidestepping the risk that the very wealth that was supposed to empower the children can end up creating a lifetime of dependency.

Not surprisingly, wealth managers see a promising market in helping families, as one put it, "manage the impact of their wealth." Firms have set up new departments, wealth-dynamics coaches have been hired, classes are offered to help teenagers gain an understanding of finance and investing, psychologists are deployed, and, of course, hefty annual fees are charged. But for any advice to be useful, the investor must be clear about his mission.

Recently, I was at a meeting where a prospect was being considered for membership. He told us that one of his investments was about to yield a huge payday, and he was pondering all the issues his additional wealth was likely to create. As he talked about what his kids were up to, I asked whether he had considered including his children in the investment itself, when it was made only a few years back, so that if it was successful they would have earned the profits directly, thereby avoiding the estate tax on those profits. More broadly, I wanted to know how much he was thinking about leaving to his children. He replied: "*I'm not planning on giving them anything. . .*" Just as I was trying not to overreact to one more lecture on tough love, he surprised me by adding, "*but I am prepared to invest everything in them.*"

For me, it was a *wow* moment. In one simple sentence this successful entrepreneur had crystallized an issue that I had been thinking about for years. He had suddenly changed the paradigm from *giving* your assets to your kids to *investing* in their future. Investing implies a partnership and a purpose. It endows the assets that you turn over to them with the expectation of a return, whether emotional, physical, or financial. Suddenly, I saw graduate school costs as investments in the future rather than expenses. I had a new filter for evaluating potential business ventures that I might fund (a yoga studio, a company), or even certain lifestyle enhancements, such as a new condominium.

A recent conversation with some extremely successful friends came to mind. One shared his pride in the fact that his kids were all out of college and more or less supporting themselves, with some working in the nonprofit world and living modestly. Finally, they were "off the family dole." Fair enough, but beginning at age 35 (or sooner, if the parents die), the children will each begin to inherit millions of dollars and may have little or no experience managing those resources and thinking about how best to use and invest them.

The second friend had a son who was grappling with what to do during an upcoming gap year created by a prestigious environmental internship that would only begin a year after he completed an environmental degree. The son was wrestling with what he should do in the meantime—work in a top consulting firm (where he might be working for the polluters) or volunteer at a world-class environmental nonprofit? The later might allow for four to six months to travel around the globe, which would give the future environmental consultant direct experience and unique insight into some of the issues he might be working on in future years, connecting him in a visceral way to his chosen path.

Having favored teaching his kids about being responsible stewards of their wealth, the second father had already transferred significant assets to his children. He had encouraged his son to use the benchmark of what would most enhance the trajectory of his career in the long term rather than being self-sufficient during the upcoming gap year.

For first-generation wealth creators who have little familiarity with inherited wealth, it is easier to fall back on the important and time-tested middle-class values that were the foundation of their own success: good work habits, personal discipline, and independence. No matter how many generations of wealth are in a family, parents should be fostering these values in their children. But the reality is that inherited wealth will burden children in relatively unique ways.

The goal should be to equip and train kids to understand the meaning of wealth and how to prudently manage it to allow for a productive and purposeful life, rather than letting it become a distraction or, worse, a force for self-destruction. It's no easy task. But grappling early on with the tensions created by these somewhat competing values and being transparent with your children about your choices can save you years of heartache.

Don't give your kids anything, but be willing to invest everything in them. See how that fits after trying it on for a while.

Consider Life Insurance

As Benjamin Franklin famously warned, "In this world nothing can be certain but death and taxes." Yet most successful entrepreneurs fail to prepare for these certainties until they are well into middle age and often only after they have sold their businesses for tens of millions of dollars. Perhaps the natural optimism that most really successful entrepreneurs have (which fuels their ability to take risks building a business) blinds them to their own mortality.

I realize that many readers, particularly young ones, are asking why they need to consider life insurance or estate planning when they don't yet have a family or an estate. But preparing early can make the difference between preserving a company after an unexpected death or losing it—and it can save literally millions of dollars for your family and the causes you care about.

Let's start with life insurance, a simple enough idea and often what ends up paying the estate taxes when an entrepreneur's journey comes to its final end. Many books have been written about the pros and cons of the seemingly limitless varieties of life insurance. Here's how I look at it: Assuming you're healthy, the younger you are when you acquire life insurance coverage, the cheaper it will be. And although life insurance can be merely a reasonable investment if you live out your full life expectancy, if you die prematurely, your investment can produce a dramatically higher return and may save you from having to liquidate assets you want to pass on to your heirs, such as businesses, buildings, farms, and even art.

In past decades, you could find many life insurance policies that would be expected to earn (or even guaranteed to earn) 7 percent per annum or more. Today, however, the returns are likely to be 5 percent or less. If your

185

life insurance policy is owned by your heirs, you can think of the 5 percent compounded return as tax free and estate free. That is nothing to sneeze at in the current environment! If you live longer than your life expectancy, the rate of return will decline. But if you die earlier, it will go up. If you die much earlier, the rate of return will go up a lot—perhaps dramatically. Imagine a $5 million life insurance policy for which the insured pays $30,000 per year in premiums. The insurance company expects to receive and invest those premiums for 20 or 30 years. If the insured dies unexpectedly in the third year, his $90,000 investment has yielded $5 million.

I am generally referring to the type of life insurance where one pays premiums for a period of years and then the insured is covered for many more years after that (or until death). Because a portion of those early payments is invested by the insurance company, the policy earns a rate of return on those payments in addition to the guaranteed benefits it pays at death. Rather than getting lost in the weeds, it is easier to just think about total payments made, total death benefits received, and the financial return implied by that stream of payments and, ultimately, receipts. Of course, there are endless insurance options, and I am not a broker (or prepared to offer insurance advice). Suffice it to say that for a young entrepreneur, the right kind of life insurance can be more valuable than it seems at first glance.

For me, life insurance is sort of like a lawn mower. If you live in an apartment or in the desert, buying one is a waste of money. But there are circumstances that are often particularly relevant to entrepreneurs—say if they own farms, real estate, private companies, or illiquid assets—where a life insurance policy can dramatically increase the net proceeds they can leave to their heirs. In many cases, the right kind of life insurance and estate structure avoids having to liquidate assets (to pay estate taxes) that one hopes to pass on to future generations. Or maybe it's just a terrible time to sell; perhaps the death of the insured has had a disastrous effect on the business because assets haven't matured to full value, or because real estate prices are in a temporary swoon. In those cases, there are few other tools that are remotely as effective as life insurance.

All this brings to mind a fable:

I live in Alexandria, Virginia. Near the Supreme Court chambers is a toll bridge across the Potomac. When in a rush, I pay the dollar toll and get home early. However, I usually drive outside the downtown section of the city and cross the Potomac on a free bridge.

This bridge was placed outside the downtown Washington, DC, area to serve a useful social service: getting drivers to drive the extra mile to help alleviate congestion during rush hour.

If I went over the toll bridge and through the barrier without paying the toll, I would be committing tax evasion.

If, however, I drive the extra mile outside the city of Washington and take the free bridge, I am using a legitimate, logical, and suitable method of tax avoidance, and I am performing a useful social service by doing so.

For my tax evasion, I should be punished. For my tax avoidance, I should be commended.

The tragedy of life is that so few people know that the free bridge even exists![1]

Most of us legitimately avoid paying taxes all the time and may not even realize it. Every person with a life insurance policy, an IRA, or who has made a tax-deductible contribution to a school, church, or any other favorite charity has crossed that free bridge of legitimate tax avoidance.

Which brings us to the much more complicated issue that so many brilliant entrepreneurs I know tend to be quite dim about: tax and estate planning.

Note

1. This story is often attributed erroneously to Louis D. Brandeis, who didn't live in Alexandria.

We Actually Live in an After-Tax World

Perhaps the most profound insight about investing (while alive), and estate planning (for later), is that most of our thinking relates to pre-tax considerations when, in fact, the net results realized are ultimately after-tax. Comparing two investments or strategies based on their pre-tax expected returns seems reasonable, but in an incredibly important number of ways, that analysis obscures what the actual comparable net results will really be. The tax impact on one investment might be dramatically different from the impact on the other, and what looks like a winning strategy in a pre-tax world ends up being the losing strategy in the after-tax world we actually live in.

Not only do relative tax rates come into play, but also the timing of when taxes are payable. The concept is so fundamental that a single example should illustrate it: Let's say that two investments have expected lives of 20 years. The first is a $10,000 bond that pays 8 percent interest each year. The interest is taxed at a combined 50 percent federal and state income tax rate. Assuming the interest can be reinvested at the same rate, the $10,000 investment grows to $21,900 after taxes. In the second case the $10,000 is invested in a stock that grows by 7 percent each year and is sold at the end of the twentieth year. The stock grows to $38,700. After paying the various taxes related to a capital gain, which total around 35 percent, the investor nets $28,650. On an after-tax basis, the stock investment that grows at 7 percent per year is worth 30 percent more than the bond investment that grows at 8 percent per year! Moreover, if an investor has a charitable intent, he could donate the appreciated stock before paying the tax and could make a $38,700 contribution, whereas he would have only had 56 percent of that amount to donate from the bond, even though the bond had grown at a higher rate. In addition, the contribution would result in a further charitable tax deduction.

It seems simple enough. But how many people would actually pick the stock that is expected to earn 7 percent instead of a bond that will appreciate 8 percent per year over the same 20-year period? And this is a relatively simple example of how easy it is to be fooled by pre-tax assessments.

Most entrepreneurs don't have to focus on this issue during the years they are building a business because the single largest asset they have is the equity in their business, which is growing tax free until the time of a sale. This is also the case for many real estate owners who don't fully appreciate the extra benefit that depreciation gives them compared to friends in other businesses, who don't have those same tax benefits. But there are opportunities to further minimize the eventual tax burden when the sale occurs or the owner dies.

Most entrepreneurs fail to structure their businesses to maximize the after-tax proceeds that might be earned from a sale or if left to their heirs, says Ron Weiner. Ron is the senior partner at a highly regarded boutique accounting firm in New York and is a master at structuring investments and estates. "Entrepreneurs are, by their very nature, highly target focused," he explains, "and for most entrepreneurs, the bull's-eye is the business."[1] The irony of such single-mindedness is that income taxes may consume about 50 percent of earned income, while estate taxes can gobble up to about 50 percent of what's left. The result: 75 percent of what you earn could be paid in taxes before your heirs will receive the remaining 25 percent. Even if the earnings are capital gains, your heirs might only inherit one-third of what you earned.

With just a modicum of estate planning, entrepreneurs could leave their heirs with much more. "The smart person," notes Ron, "generally can solve problems for themselves that the wise person would have avoided in the first place."

Wise estate planning can also ensure that your wealth will generate greater social benefits. For example, in 1998 I knew I would be selling my interests in a series of real estate partnerships, along with my share of the company that managed those partnerships. Prior to the sale, I was able to donate my interest in the management company to my foundation so that when the sale eventually occurred, the proceeds would be realized by the foundation. As a result, the foundation has been able to grant millions of dollars to philanthropic projects that otherwise would never have been funded—and it didn't have to wait until I died to do it.

Some cynics will argue that such tax schemes are partly responsible for our high government deficit, but I don't think the evidence supports that charge.

Those dollars saved from taxes were invested, and our family foundation has now granted multiples of those saved dollars to projects that will improve education, enhance our national security, and fight climate change. Socialist governments around the world levy higher taxes to pay for most of those things, but that is not the American way. For me and many passionate philanthropists, the amount we pay in taxes *plus* the amount of charitable contributions we make far exceeds the taxes we would likely pay (if the government took care of such social needs, so we didn't have to), even with higher tax rates.

Here is one of Ron's examples of how tax planning can make a huge difference: The foundation on which much of America's wealth has been built is equity ownership of stocks or companies. The current tax code incentivizes private business owners who are ready to exit their businesses to sell them to their employees through a legal structure known as an employee stock ownership plan (ESOP). In certain cases, the seller who sells to an ESOP can avoid paying gains taxes at the time of the sale if his stake in the business is exchanged for other investments. Of course, when those new investments are eventually sold, the full tax will be payable. In the meantime, however, those pre-tax proceeds can be reinvested to generate additional returns from the new portfolio. How many more entrepreneurs, ready to sell, would go out of their way to enhance their employees' futures if they knew they would receive a significant tax benefit for doing so?

Here's another benefit if you've been thinking about bringing children into the business as partners. If the parents own the business outright, it is quite possible that estate taxes can either force the sale of a business or diminish the value of the portion of the business inherited by the children. But if the children had been part owners of the business from the beginning, or even bought a part of the business when it was worth much less, then the estate tax on the portion of the business remaining in the parent's estate at the time of death will be far less. If a wise plan for transferring a family business to the children is put in place and enough time elapses to execute it, a significant portion of the estate taxes that would have otherwise been payable will be avoided, and there will be far less disruption to the family's business than if the parent's death forces a sale or a liquidation. For some owners, considerations of what their heirs will inherit are secondary to other issues more relevant during their lifetime (such as retaining absolute control and access to all one's assets, although these issues also can be addressed). However, reducing the net value of proceeds ultimately received by children, other heirs, or beneficiaries by 25 to 50 percent is something that should only be done consciously and after much thought, and certainly not by default. These are just a few very simple examples, but there are many other structures and techniques that minimize taxes and maximize what heirs and charities can reap from an entrepreneur's success. But regardless, unless you start thinking about after-tax returns (income, gains, and inheritance), you will be focusing on the wrong ball.

Why am I dwelling on this? Because, as Albert Einstein purportedly said, "The strongest force in the universe is the power of compounding." By way of example, let's say the patriarch of a family died in 1986 and the three buildings in his estate were worth $1 million. Let's simplify our example and stipulate that the estate taxes were 50 percent of the $1 million, or $500,000. (I am not including the current lifetime exemption, so consider this a marginal analysis.)

Fortunately, the patriarch had taken out a $500,000 life insurance policy three years before his death, on which he paid $15,000 per year in premiums (this patriarch was young, so the premiums were low). Without that insurance, there would have been an additional $45,000 in the estate, which would have totaled just over $1 million before estate taxes were paid. Now, however, the $500,000 of insurance proceeds (because the insurance was held in an insurance trust for the children, and yes, I am avoiding discussing how the trust was funded) fully pays the estate tax. And the heirs get to keep the buildings without the need to encumber the buildings by borrowing money to pay the estate taxes.

Thirty years go by. Because the buildings were kept intact, the son took over the portfolio and grew it aggressively: the assets have grown at a 14 percent compounded rate, which turns $1 into $50 over a 30-year period. That portfolio of three buildings that was worth $1 million in 1986 is now 20 buildings worth $50 million. This kind of appreciation has actually been available to top-tier real estate entrepreneurs in gateway cities such as New York in the last generation.

Contrast that with the same $1.05 million estate with no life insurance. Estate taxes turn the $1.05 million into $522,000. The cash to make the estate tax payment was generated by borrowing money in the form of mortgages against the three buildings, which prevents the son from growing the portfolio as aggressively. Worse still, one of the buildings lost its sole tenant in the crash of 1987, and the bank foreclosed on the mortgage and repossessed the building. After many years of hard work, and after making up for the loss of that one important building, the son is still able to deliver a compounded growth rate of 9 percent. (Who wouldn't want that today?) Over 30 years, that 9 percent turns $1 into $13 dollars, which turns that $522,000 estate into $6.8 million.

Fifty million dollars is more than seven times as much as $6.8 million. All because of a life insurance policy that cost $45,000 over the final three years of the patriarch's life.

"I am amazed," Ron says, "that when it comes to their estate planning, some very astute entrepreneurs approach it as if they were in first grade." Emotional issues related to mortality are hard to deal with. They paralyze some people from doing what is so clearly in their family's best interest.

The lesson that our entrepreneurs learn is that the sooner they can switch their focus from, as Ron put it, "the bull's-eye of their business" to an evolved, broader perspective about family asset accumulation, the sooner they will be en route to maximizing what their heirs or charities will inherit (if that's important to them).

The key to that transition is recognizing that you really live in an after-tax world. Keeping that in mind will change your approach to almost every investment you consider.

As I write this in the spring of 2017, President Donald Trump is indicating he will eliminate estate taxes. No doubt, this will render estate plans that were established at material cost unnecessary, and many parents will lament the costs already incurred to establish estate plans that will become irrelevant, or unnecessarily costly. I am not sure it is any different than the cost of car insurance that is "wasted" when one doesn't have an accident. If present trends in the United States continue, federal budget deficits are unlikely to go away anytime soon. It remains likely that future administrations will rely once again on the estate tax, not just to raise revenue but because of matters of tax equity. Better to use the current period, if estate taxes are eliminated, to shift assets to your kids, so if the tax is reinstituted, the transfers will have already been made.

Note

1. Ron Weiner, interview (September 2016).

STAGE 6

Making It Meaningful

Members of Tiger 21 are achieving amazing things in the world of philanthropy—but not all of them, to be honest. Some find discussions about philanthropy to be off-putting. They argue, in effect, "I've given at the office," meaning that they've created lots of jobs or paid lots of taxes and so helped strengthen their communities. To be sure, creating jobs and being a good corporate citizen is important. But is it enough?

Most of our members would think not. And thanks to the power of their peers, they're often changing minds. Here's how Charlie Garcia describes the dynamic: "For the first time in their careers, members are surrounded by peers who are just as wealthy as they are (or more so), who tell them the truth. 'What are you doing? You're worth more money than you could ever spend, and you're still working 21-hour days and have three kids you don't really even know? Pat yourself on the back: you made it. Now start focusing on something that is going to bring you fulfillment.'"

More often than not, after the big liquidity event, entrepreneurs start to rebuild family ties that had been frayed while they were single-mindedly focused on building their business. Next, they start to think about the causes they wish they'd had time and capital to support during the years they were a bit absent. I've often observed that when an entrepreneur does commit to donating money and time to an issue, cause, or institution they care about, they wish that they'd done it sooner.

In this last section of the book, we will look at ways that entrepreneurship can help make this planet a more just and more prosperous one.

LESSON 38

Apply Your Skills to Solve Social Problems

In 2012, I had a visit from a supremely talented entrepreneur whom I'd lost touch with a decade before. He wanted to talk to me about something, but he hadn't said what on the phone when we set up the appointment.

Sometimes I can be insensitive. Ask me a question, and I spit out an answer like a human gumball machine. So when Gary Mendell asked me how I was doing, I told him about my various business and health travails, including a bout of cancer I had suffered through since we last met. When I finally got around to asking Gary what he was up to, I noticed the sadness in his eyes. As he answered my question, he started crying. As I listened to him, I did too.

He told me that his son Brian, the oldest of his five kids, had battled drug addiction.[1] Gary tried everything. He sent Brian to treatment programs, wilderness programs, therapeutic boarding schools, and halfway houses. Brian's struggles were at the center of his life—and the life of the whole Mendell family—for a decade.

Then, on October 20, 2011, Gary received the news that every parent dreads. Brian, who had been clean for 13 months, wrote a loving note explaining that sobriety wasn't working for him and that he didn't want to keep hurting people. At age 25, he hanged himself.

Gary was devastated. He wondered what he might have done better as a parent. And he felt very much alone. Gary told me that there had been another kid in their family's town, Mikey, who'd had cancer. There were fundraisers to support the search for a cure for Mikey's disease. When he died, the town mourned him and made sure he would be remembered with plaques and memorials. Mikey's parents found comfort in all that support and love from their community.

No one held fundraisers for Brian's disease. No one embraced him during his battle. And after his death, the only people outside his family and closest friends who rallied to Gary's side were Brian's friends, some of whom were grappling with the same demons. Many told Gary how much Brian had helped them, some telling Gary that Brian had saved their life.

Gary wanted to do something to honor Brian's memory, but all he could do was lie in bed crying. His wife had framed the Serenity Prayer and placed it on his nightstand. Gary told me the only thing that had kept him alive during those first few weeks was reading the first sentence over and over again: "God, grant me the serenity to accept the things I cannot change." As time went on, he began to read and think about the second sentence, "the courage to change the things I can." With his wife's patience and encouragement, he decided to take action. What he accomplished is a lesson in what a brilliant entrepreneur can achieve when he puts his talents to use in the world of philanthropy.

Gary's father grew up poor in Bridgeport, Connecticut, and moved to Florida, where he met his wife and found a job selling used cars. But before he really settled down in the Sunshine State, he got a phone call from a hometown buddy who told him that his family had just bought a local hamburger stand. If Gary's father would put in $500 and run the business, he said, he could have half of it.

Growing up in the 1960s, Gary and his brother, Steve, spent much of their free time working at the hamburger stand. Eventually, both went to Cornell's School of Hotel Administration. Steve got a job in hotel market research and Gary went to work for the Ponderosa Steakhouse chain, where soon enough he was managing six restaurants and loving it. Then he got a call from his father's partners: Gary could have a share of a hamburger restaurant in Fairfield, Connecticut, if he agreed to run the place.

"When you have an opportunity to own something," Gary says, "you grab it." After his restaurant opened he was out looking for a second location when, over a Thanksgiving dinner, he decided to team up with his brother to move into the hotel business. This was the early 1980s, when small entrepreneurs were discovering the power of computers. Mastering the Lotus 1-2-3 spreadsheet program, Gary developed a pricing model for valuing hotels while Steve began searching for investment opportunities.

They zeroed in on a Marriott hotel in Connecticut, two miles from what was then General Electric's headquarters. Thanks to a pitch backed up by Gary's pricing model, the Mendell brothers lined up 80 investors at $107,000 each. "We took a $320,000 fee up front," Gary recalls. "It was like a billion dollars to us. We got an office, an assistant, and two $20 desks." Next, Steve found a piece of land in Princeton, New Jersey. Gary rounded up more investors, and they built an $11 million hotel. When it opened, it was instantly worth $15 million.

By 1990, they had half a dozen hotels. Then a recession hit. They made a deal with the largest hotel-consulting firm in the United States to purchase the rights to half its international business, and Steve moved to London to build the business. Gary stuck with their hotels here in the States and cut expenses to get them through the tough financial climate.

In 1992, Gary saw that occupancies were slowly starting to rise, and he was one of the first to jump back in to buy hotels. He convinced investors to back him, and, one by one, he acquired four hotels for $60 million. Within a year those hotels were worth $80 million. Then Prudential called: If the company allocated $100 million for buying hotel properties, would the Mendell brothers partner with them?

Yes, they would!

Their hotel portfolio ballooned, and in 1997, the Mendells and Prudential sold the portfolio to Starwood Lodging Trust for $300 million. Gary was named president and elected to its board of trustees. It was exciting for a short while. In rapid succession Starwood bought the Westin hotel chain and then Sheraton too, but Gary ultimately felt like a small piece of an increasingly large company and decided to leave.

Like many who have sold their businesses, Gary suddenly realized that he was alone and stuck with a new job he wasn't prepared for: wealth manager. Quickly, Gary realized he was not as rich as he'd thought.

When Gary signed the contract with Starwood to purchase his portfolio, his share of the sale was for many millions of Starwood stock, which then doubled (on paper) within a few months because of a rise in Starwood's stock. But by the time of his departure about a year later, the stock had fallen dramatically, and when he liquidated his holdings, taxes took a big portion of what was left. He quickly realized that his resources, when invested passively, could not produce as much income as he had expected.

Note: In a low-interest-rate environment like the one we have been in for years, most entrepreneurs—who sell businesses for a multiple of earnings, pay taxes on the sale, and then earn a modest return on the passively invested net proceeds—find they are earning dramatically lower income after a sale, although arguably *with less risk. In many cases, this turns out to be an unexpected, and unwelcome, surprise. In simple terms (as but one example), if a business was earning $2 million per year and sold for 7 times earnings, or $14 million, then taxes might take $3 million and leave the entrepreneur with $11 million. That money invested passively at 3 percent might generate $330,000 of annual earnings—or about one-sixth of the annual income the entrepreneur was earning before the sale! No matter how rich you are, if your income drops by over 80 percent, it can have a dramatic impact, and if you had not fully thought this through before the sale, it can easily snatch a deep sense of failure from the jaws of success.*

To be sure, 99 percent of Americans would not shed a tear for Gary. But after you've sold your business for more money than you ever dreamed of, that kind of sticker shock made Gary feel unexpectedly vulnerable. Then the terrorist attacks of September 11, 2001, sparked historic declines in the stock market, shrinking the value of Gary's portfolio by a third. While many saw only fear and disarray in the markets, Gary saw an opportunity to buy valuable hotel properties at bargain prices. Still in his early forties and weary of working on his golf game and worrying about how long his money would last, he partnered again with his brother and used their credibility in the hotel sector to attract institutional investors. Over the next decade, they built a $2 billion owner/operator colossus of more than 40 upscale and luxury hotels and resorts. As chairman and CEO, Gary was at the top of his game.

Then Brian died. Gary had a vision for how he wanted to honor his son's memory based on something that Brian had once said to him: "Someday, society will recognize that I have a disease and I am trying my hardest." Gary wanted to hasten that day by using the $65,000 friends had donated in Brian's name and whatever it took of his own money to create a small charity dedicated to removing the stigma of addiction, which he would call "Brian's Wish." But first he needed a strategy.

He turned over the management of his real estate company to his top executives so that he could devote himself full-time to his startup. He immersed himself in the literature on addiction. He was struck by a few facts. "I had no idea how big this was," he said. Twenty-two million Americans are addicted to drugs and alcohol; that's 1 in 10 above the age of 12. Addiction is the third largest cause of death after heart disease and cancer, killing 135,000 Americans every year. Every day, 375 people die. Every day, 375 families are shattered forever. Who knew?

He was also struck by the fact that the vast majority of the research on effective prevention and treatment programs resided in medical journals and wasn't being implemented by our communities or health-care system. It wasn't that there weren't important solutions to address the problem, but rather that there were programs that had been designed and tested, and their efficacy documented, but they just weren't being funded or implemented!

As a veteran entrepreneur who had built a multibillion-dollar business from scratch in a decade, he knew he was staring at a huge gap in the market. Known treatments that could prevent, manage, and cure various forms of addiction weren't being used. A rudderless treatment industry was missing out on important research that would increase their success. There was no national organization, like the National Heart Association or the American Cancer Society, dedicated to education, research funding, public policy advocacy, and support for treatment of addiction. Without that, the unjust stigma of addiction would be impossible to overturn.

Gary knew what he had to do. Adding $5 million of his own money to the donations, he launched Brian's Wish, later named Shatterproof, the first national organization committed to protecting our loved ones from addiction and ending the stigma around this disease.

Shatterproof continues to grow, pursuing goals for the next 20 years that match Gary's own ambition: to reduce by 50 percent the number of people addicted to alcohol and other substances while also halving the number of deaths and addiction's cost to society. This is estimated by the National Institutes of Health to be more than $417 billion each year. To achieve such enormous results, Gary realized that Shatterproof would have to be a large, national organization. Running Shatterproof like a business, Gary has positioned it to save tens of thousands of lives. He is well down the path to reaching his goals.

What problem keeps you awake at night?

Note

1. Gary Mendell, interview (November 14, 2016).

Leverage Public/Private Support for Social Entrepreneurship

We met Ron Bruder in Lesson 11 when I shared the story of his remarkable entrepreneurial and philanthropic career. Ron's daughter worked near the World Trade Center on September 11, 2001. It wasn't until the end of that nightmarish day that Ron got word that she was safe. Before the relief had worn off, he decided to devote his entrepreneurial talent—and $10 million of his own money—to creating an organization that would become Education for Employment, or EFE (www.efe.org), which could "foster hope, stability, and prosperity in the Middle East and North Africa" and just maybe prevent the next 9/11, or something even worse.

But how? Ron spent much of the next four years traveling, searching for an answer. With the help of some of the region's top thinkers and leaders, he identified youth unemployment as the biggest problem. (The region has the highest unemployment rate in the world.) So Ron, a Jew from Brooklyn who had made a fortune building retail malls and cleaning up and developing brownfields, set out to change the economies of the Middle East and North Africa. Job training would be the key.

"Initially, I went to Washington," he recalls. "People laughed at me."[1] But it wasn't the first time that experts had waved off one of Ron's innovative ideas. Patiently and strategically, he began to piece together relationships with business and social leaders from Morocco to Yemen. He cajoled, networked, and occasionally used his money. And then in 2006 he disengaged from all his business activities to devote his financial and operational resources to what he considered his "new business."

Since 2006, EFE has trained more than 40,000 disadvantaged young Arabs, teaching job skills and how to search for employment, placing more than 10,500 of them with the organization's 2,100-plus employment partners, including *Fortune* 500 companies as well as small and medium-sized local businesses. In 2011, millions of young people took to the streets in the region's capitals during the Arab Spring, confirming Ron's vision that unemployment was a central problem in the region. *Time* magazine named him one of its 100 most influential people in the world. In 2012, he was named Social Entrepreneur of the Year at the World Economic Forum in Davos, Switzerland.

"When I go to a graduation and look at a young girl's eyes," says Ron, "and I see how she's been empowered, or her life has been transformed, I see how her family has been transformed, I say, 'Yesss! This is why I love what I'm doing.' This is the most exciting thing I've done in my life."

Ron will not lack for graduations to attend. Structured as a social franchise, EFE was built for long-term impact, establishing local EFE nonprofit affiliates in eight countries to date, including Egypt, Jordan, Morocco, Palestine, Tunisia, Yemen, Saudi Arabia, and Algeria, backed up by support hubs in the United States, Spain, and the United Arab Emirates.

Ron and Gary Mendell (Lesson 38) followed in the footsteps of America's great entrepreneur philanthropists—from Andrew Carnegie to Bill Gates—who transferred their business skills and passion to building large nonprofit organizations with a mission to improve the world. They are making a huge difference.

Note

1. Ron Bruder, interview (November 8, 2016).

Seek Double-Bottom-Line Returns

Social entrepreneurship is on the rise. Companies that pursue socially relevant goals as part of their mission (no matter where their owners find themselves on the political spectrum or the social divide) offer investors the potential to generate double-bottom-line results, by which I mean a financial return and also a social benefit. The standard explanation for the recent growth in social entrepreneurship is twofold. First, foundations are eager to use their investments to attract capital from private investors, and second, millennials are taking their social values into the marketplace. I would add a third reason, which is that the markets are the best source of the massive amounts of capital that are needed to address the mounting global challenges of poverty, education, malaria, food security, and more.

All our philanthropies combined don't have enough money to make a dent in these problems. Total annual philanthropic giving in the United States is around $320 billion. That's a lot of money. But when you take out funds used for education and religion, that $320 billion gets a whole lot smaller. Meanwhile, institutional investors in the United States, Canada, and Europe—pension funds, insurance companies, banks, sovereign wealth funds, investment funds, hedge funds, private equity funds—have *$75 trillion in assets* under management.

We need to leverage as much of that capital as possible. I have been doing my part by investing in the fight against global climate change, which

I believe is one of the most challenging and potentially devastating problems we face (but sadly not the only one). I also invest significant resources trying to help better understand and combat terrorism and weapons of mass destruction, two other serious and immediate dangers, but climate change is my top focus. Like the majority of Americans, I believe that climate change is both real and man-made. I also believe, along with many U.S. corporate leaders and the Pentagon, that it poses a serious and growing threat to our economic future and our national security.

Climate change has been accelerated by private investment in fossil fuels and agriculture. Fighting it will take an investment mechanism that can scale equally quickly to finance the technological innovations in wind farms, solar panels, batteries, electric cars, geothermal heating and cooling, and other game changers that have the potential to reduce carbon dioxide emissions while creating new industries and jobs.

I have discovered that my capital can have an impact on the problem and also generate financial returns. I have also discovered that social entrepreneurship is not easy.

Back in 1989, I invested in Solar Outdoor Lighting Inc. (now Sol Inc.), a Florida company that manufactured the first generation of solar streetlights. The company needed capital, and I was fascinated by the idea of a wireless source of clean-energy lighting. Sol kept needing money, and I kept supporting it to keep it alive. By 2007, I owned 90 percent of the company. It wasn't generating any returns, but I was committed to the company's mission and the impact it could have on the environment. In that regard, I considered my funding of Sol's losses as part of my charitable giving, although I did hold out hope that one day it would turn the corner and, by helping to address a significant global challenge, would also become profitable.

Three years later, during the aftermath of the earthquake that killed 200,000 people and turned the city of Port-au-Prince, Haiti, into a field of rubble, Sol's products saved lives in a way that allowed me to viscerally understand the impact that lighting can have. Our team was on one of the first planes in after the earthquake. We installed half a million dollars' worth of outdoor solar lights at the airport and at emergency medical clinics and feeding stations. We put lights at search and rescue sites, which enabled around-the-clock efforts to pull people out of the rubble. This was not a matter of just writing a check. We had personnel on the ground and had to provide armed protection because Haiti was in total chaos. But few people realize that when a disaster strikes, without light, emergency feeding, medical, and rescue crews can't work once the sun goes down.

It's difficult to convey how satisfying this felt. After that, I went on a quest for impact. After the 2011 tsunami disaster in Japan, we lit up a pier so local fishermen could begin fishing at 4 a.m. and get their lives back together.

But there was a problem: We were doing good, but we weren't making money as a business, and my goal was to do both. Almost everyone I trusted advised me to sell the company—my family, friends, and the smart investors I confided in at Tiger 21. Even my shrink told me to sell.

But I couldn't do it. I felt I was on the right track—at least for me.

My persistence was not irrational. Solar and wind power were coming on strong. Innovations in solar panels and battery storage were increasing efficiency and decreasing costs in dramatic ways, and prices were coming down. I made another investment in solar, this time in a public Canadian company that manufactured solar-powered landing lights for airports in developing countries and in places where the military needed to build an airport and get it operational quickly. The company also designed and built solar-powered marine navigational aids (the red and green flashing lights atop buoys in all of America's Coast Guard–maintained waterways)—and it competed with Sol in the outdoor lighting business (in a minor way). It took five years, a lot of capital, and a lot of patience, but in 2014 we merged the two companies and put the combined entity on a path to profitability.

I partnered with a talented CEO who put together a great team. Our company, Carmanah Technologies, which I now chair, is seeing results on both its bottom lines, impact and profit. Even more amazingly, as Carmanah gained momentum, I recouped decades of losses (at least on paper). Carmanah has gone from an enterprise value of $6 million at its low point in October 2013 to over $100 million at the end of 2015. Its stock has grown from a low of $0.90 per share to around $4 in the same time period. For a short while, we actually reached a high of over $7 per share!

Of course, what goes up can come down. But for me, personally, my belief in solar has been vindicated. So has my optimism and hanging in there for so long. When Carmanah finally built a track record of growing profitability, people were congratulating me on my 24-month Carmanah success as if it were an overnight sensation. Congratulations are certainly in order, but by my count, it was a 27-year sensation.

As an alternative energy investor, I see amazing market opportunities. Solar power is already competitive in 11 states; the prediction is that it will be competitive in 28 states by the end of 2017. Europe and Asia are embracing solar so quickly that the International Energy Agency (IEA) is predicting that by 2050 solar could be the single biggest source of power, delivering as much as 27 percent of electricity worldwide. Solar panels will continue to get cheaper, while their efficiency will only grow.

In solar lighting, where I have historically focused, we have reached a magical inflection point. In the last decade, the cost of solar power has dropped by 90 percent, from $5 per watt to $0.50 per watt, while the efficiency of light sources has grown from about 20 lumens per watt to 150 lumens per watt in today's LED fixtures. That means that the $5.00 that used to buy 1 watt of power, which created 20 lumens of light output, today buys 10 watts of power, which produces 1,500 lumens of light output. That is a 75-fold increase in cost effectiveness.

While those efficiencies only affect part of the entire system, that is why we can produce a solar-powered commercial parking lot light today for $800 that is better in every respect than what we sold for $5,000 just a few years ago. For a growing number of new parking lots in North America, solar-powered lighting is both cheaper and better. The solar lights perform as well as or better than their grid-tied equivalents, but they save all the trenching and copper wiring (and often repaving) that grid-tied lights require. Better still, the energy for the solar light is free forever and produces no carbon dioxide pollution.

From a political perspective, what is so amazing is that solar-powered street and parking lot lights are the only alternative energy investment I am aware of that saves money from day one. No tax incentives or green banks or subsidies needed—just a purchase order.

I am also invested in other development-stage companies in the solar field, but it is rougher going there. One exciting development was solar roof tiles. We had made a lot of progress, but at the time of this writing, it looks like Tesla may have leapfrogged over our company. To my way of thinking, all the better. Progress in the industry is vital, no matter who gets there first.

I have also completed an investment in a wave-energy company that is in its early days. Until recently, I had not realized that ocean waves can produce dramatically more power than the winds circling the earth. If this technology proves itself, offshore wave farms will be cheaper and generate far more power per dollar invested than the growing number of offshore wind farms, and put yet another nail in the coffin of the fossil fuels that are destroying the planet.

As excited as I am about these latest alternative investments, I've had my disappointments. Right now, I am writing off what appeared to be an exciting investment in a new battery company that had the potential to change the equation with electricity storage—the holy grail for a smart alternative energy future. We're hardly alone in our optimism about the opportunities in battery storage, but this particular investment failed.

The alternative energy future is spawning all sorts of other new technologies and new businesses, providing plenty of investment opportunities. All that capital will create lots of new jobs, demolishing the myth that alternative energy solutions are job killers. Yes, coal miners will be out of work, but they can be trained for better and safer jobs in clean energy industries or all the other businesses that will flourish in a clean energy economy.

At the end of 2015, 208,859 Americans were working in the solar industry, which was adding jobs nearly 12 times faster than the rest of the economy, according to a recent state-by-state survey. Add the jobs created by other renewables—wind and hydropower, biomass, and geothermal—plus the jobs created to increase energy efficiency in buildings, appliances, vehicles, and mass transportation, and you have 3.8 million jobs, according to the latest data from the Bureau of Labor Statistics. And there are many more to come.

It has never been easier to create socially responsible companies: 27 states have enacted new laws for *benefit corporations* to allow firms to be held accountable not simply to their shareholders but other constituencies impacted by their work, such as communities and employees.

If you aspire to be a successful entrepreneur who would also like to make a difference, it's probably time for you to join the new and growing vanguard of proud double-bottom-line capitalists. Future generations will be glad you did.

Conclusion

When I decided to leave my secure career to strike out on a project that even seasoned developers thought was risky—they used much spicier language—I didn't think of myself as an entrepreneur. I just knew in my bones that I had to go for that first deal in Jersey City. No amount of stability was going to keep me from taking my shot. And the more I heard that it couldn't be done or that I was being completely unrealistic or living in some kind of fantasy, the more determined I became to prove the skeptics wrong.

To me, this penchant for risk-taking and the desire to be my own boss seemed as natural as breathing.

Now I know better. If the past four decades of my professional life have taught me anything, it's that entrepreneurs are a completely different species. What makes us tick would induce vertigo in most others—even those who are high achievers in the business world.

Most businesspeople pay lip service to Steve Jobs's "think different" motto, but I suspect that even the most iconoclastic of them only step outside the box with great trepidation, fearing the wrath of their bosses or boards. In contrast, almost all the business founders I know can't help but think different. It almost seems that they are wired that way.

It turns out there's a very good chance that they actually are. Increasingly—and excitingly—cutting-edge research by neuroscientists and psychologists is showing that the differences between entrepreneurs and traditional business-people aren't just anecdotal. Scott Shane, a professor at Case Western University and the author of *Born Entrepreneurs, Born Leaders: How Your Genes Affect Your Work Life*, has found that 37 to 48 percent of the tendency to be an entrepreneur is genetic.[1] He and his colleagues also found that particular traits—open-mindedness, for example—are encoded in our genes and that they tend to indicate if a person is cut out to be an entrepreneur.

James Koch, the author of *Born, Not Made: The Entrepreneurial Personality*, has echoed these findings. Koch's studies have found what anyone who has known an entrepreneur intimately will attest, that they are high energy, decisive, and unafraid to ruffle feathers. And no amount of business school courses can teach a person to have these qualities.

And as I learned when researching Lesson 20, entrepreneurs access different parts of their brain than most other business leaders do. So many of the traits that help entrepreneurs thrive would guarantee their failure in other lines of work. While a number of the successful entrepreneurs I know distinguished themselves in the corporate world, law, engineering, and even academia, an amazingly significant number are not fit to succeed in traditional careers. I realized this about myself fairly early on: The idea of working for someone—anyone—who might remind me of my father's intolerance and inflexibility caused me tremendous anxiety.

This sort of thinking is not at all unique among the entrepreneurs I know. Maybe they're not dogged by a tough relationship with a parent, but by their attention deficit disorder or dyslexia or other learning disabilities. But the very act of overcoming such challenges was what steeled them for their careers as self-starters.

While many readers of this book may be grappling with the choice of whether to become an entrepreneur, some will eventually realize that they have no choice. For whatever reason—family background, learning style, or a deeply independent streak—fitting into a formal organizational structure just won't work.

Luckily, there are more ways to make it as an entrepreneur today than there have ever been. Yes, there's Silicon Valley, a powerful magnet for ambitious young people passionate about high-tech opportunities. But I've found that often the most enticing option for those just starting out is that of social entrepreneurship.

Back in 1970, the economist Milton Friedman famously warned do-gooder CEOs that "the social responsibility of business is to increase profit." I bought that argument myself in the early years of my career. Today's young people don't—and they shouldn't.[2]

According to a recent survey of 5,000 millennials across 18 countries, most believe that the number one priority of business is "to improve society." These purpose-driven young people, eager to bring their values to the market, have the option of launching careers as social entrepreneurs and impact investors with the mission of profiting from a double bottom line: benefiting society while earning exciting returns.

Social entrepreneurship is just the latest manifestation of what I see as the most valuable attribute of the entrepreneurial DNA: the ability to create productive businesses and organizations out of nothing but an idea. Historically, entrepreneurs created the vast majority of the private-sector jobs that have underpinned our economy since the country's founding, contributing mightily to the steepest rise in standards of living ever seen.

I have faith that they will continue to be the engine of the American economy. But even a congenital optimist like me is shaken by the bleak economic forecast these days.

Over the past 15 years, according to the U.S. Bureau of Economic Analysis (BEA), real income growth for the bottom fifth of the population has declined essentially to zero (0.1 percent). Half of this decline has been attributed to slower overall global economic growth; half to rising income inequality. According to BEA data, we had gone 10 straight years without 3 percent growth in gross domestic product (GDP) by the end of 2015. The last time such a poor growth period was reported was from 1930 to 1933, the middle of the Great Depression. As I write this conclusion in early 2017, GDP growth stands at 1.4 percent, although the first quarter of the Trump administration seems to be even worse.

What's going on? Explanations vary, but the one that has received the most attention lately is *secular stagnation*—a term that was coined during the Great Depression by the economist Alvin Hansen to describe long-term stagnation.[3]

The Harvard economist and former Secretary of the Treasury Lawrence Summers has argued that this stagnation is a demand-side problem—a combination of a global savings glut and low inflation resulting in weak aggregate demand in the high-income regions of the world, such as the United States and Europe.

But the economist Robert Gordon, in his celebrated book, *The Rise and Fall of American Growth: The U.S. Standard of Living Since the Civil War*, argues that, contra Summers, stagnation is in fact a "supply side" problem: the result of the slow pace of technological change. He believes that the string of "only once" inventions that transformed the world's standard of living in the 100-year period between 1870 and 1970—running water, toilets, electricity, telephones, railroads, automobiles, air travel, television, computers, and antibiotics, to name a few—has all but run its course. He doubts that future scientific and technological breakthroughs will have the impact of the ones that emerged during that unique century.

I'm inclined to disagree *with almost every bone in my body*! I believe the ambitions and energies of American entrepreneurs will ultimately prove Gordon wrong. But I can't ignore the fact that at this very moment in history—when the innovation and technological change that will generate more jobs and restart our economic engine is most crucial—entrepreneurs appear to be an endangered species in America.

"Business deaths now exceed business births for the first time in the thirty-year history of our data," wrote Ian Hathaway and Robert E. Litan, who analyzed the latest U.S. Census Bureau data for a 2014 Brookings report titled "Declining Business Dynamism in the United States."[4] They also found that the startup rate—the number of new firms as a proportion of all firms—fell by nearly half between 1978 and 2011.

Pointing to those same Census Bureau figures in a 2015 essay, "American Entrepreneurship: Dead or Alive?" the chairman and CEO of Gallup, Jim Clifton, noted that despite the usual boosterism from politicians on both sides of the aisle, America's standing among developed nations for startups wasn't anything to boast about: Hungary, Denmark, Finland, New Zealand, Sweden, Israel, and Italy all had higher relative rates of startup activity than the U.S. did.[5] Even the much-fabled tech sector has seen its startup rate decline at a precipitous rate since the dot-com crash of the early 2000s.[6] This sudden shortage of new businesses, argues Clifton, "is our single most important economic problem."

For all those business school programs in entrepreneurship, entrepreneurial activity is clearly on the decline. The number of business owners under 30 is at a 24-year low—no surprise, considering that 48 percent fall in the net worth of under-30 households since the beginning of the 2007–2008 financial crisis. Banks pulled back from lending at the outset of the crisis, and they are still holding back. Even venture capitalists have become more cautious. By the end of 2015, they were directing their money into "the most mature private companies," such as Snapchat and Lyft, leaving funding for startups at a four-year low, a slowdown that persisted through the first quarter of 2016.[7]

Add to all that the heavy debt burden from college and graduate school that today's young people are carrying, and it's no wonder that so many millennials are scared away from starting their own companies. In a recent annual study by a Babson College business professor, 41 percent of Americans 24–35 years old who saw an opportunity to start a business confessed that "fear of failure" would keep them from doing so, up from about 24 percent in 2001.[8] That is more than a worrisome number. It's a threat to the future of the American economy.

In his most recent book, *Thank You for Being Late*, Thomas Friedman talks about the extraordinary opportunities that have been created by the technological revolution we are witnessing.[9] The combination of ever-cheaper and more powerful computing power, cheaper and more plentiful storage, almost free communications, and networks that connect almost everyone is empowering individuals from around the world to start businesses that can scale globally. For the relatively lucky few, these trends create opportunities for advancement never seen before in the history of humanity. But the fact remains that many of these advances are replacing human labor with automation, and that the technologies riding this trend are sucking investment capital away from other startups that might produce more jobs per dollar of capital invested.

Combine the decline in the growth of entrepreneurialism, the disproportionate allocation of venture capital to exciting technology startups that do not produce a lot of jobs (on a relative basis), and the growing replacement of jobs by machines and technology, and you have a perfect storm of forces hammering the working class. As young technology entrepreneurs create multibillion-dollar fortunes overnight, the overall economy is growing at an anemic rate, and the working and middle class, understandably, feel like they are getting a raw deal.

These negative trends have broad implications beyond simple economics. In a famous speech at the end of his presidency, Dwight Eisenhower talked about the pillars of national security: He described it as a three-legged stool. While military strength is certainly one of its legs, economic strength and the strength of civil society were the other two. A nation can't be strong or safe without a strong economy. We saw that with the downfall of the Soviet Union. And we cannot have a strong economy and a healthy middle class (and thus a stable civil society) without vibrant entrepreneurial activity.

You need only look to Israel for an example of the economic strength that it takes to underwrite its disproportionate need for defense expenditures. If Israel were not a *startup nation*, its ability to underwrite its security needs would have been severely compromised. The discussion of the state of our civil society is a subject for another book, but when an economy is in relative decline (or just not growing sufficiently), or the spoils of success are not equitably shared across the society, civil institutions can become an accelerant of discord. If the drift of political feeling turns against the entrepreneurial job creators who can do the most to fuel the engines of growth, it will be that much harder to rekindle the momentum that we need to meet the challenges of the future.

If Eisenhower were alive today, I suspect he would be horrified that the political class is doing so little to help reverse these negative trends. Many entrepreneurs—across the political spectrum, I hasten to add—believe it is harder to start a successful company today than it has been in prior periods of our history—thanks to the rules and regulations that keep coming out of Washington.

Recent reports on the headwinds that keep entrepreneurs from getting their businesses off the ground suggest they are correct. In their Brookings report on declining business dynamism, for example, Hathaway and Litan note that a growing number of successful businesses are pulling up the ladder on potential competitors by lobbying legislatures to create cumbersome employment regulations that limit the ability of engineers and other technical workers to move from job to job.[10]

Admittedly, non-compete clauses have served my own businesses well, ensuring that the jobs of existing employees are not put at risk (not to mention me and my investments) by other employees jumping ship with our proprietary ideas. But I can't help but wonder if the fact that California has basically deemed non-compete clauses unenforceable is part of the reason that Silicon Valley is booming.

Professional associations have persuaded state legislators to establish strict certification requirements to work or start businesses, preventing, for example, nurse practitioners and dental hygienists from performing certain services outside a traditional doctor's or dentist's office. "In the 1950s, only 70 professions had licensing requirements; by 2008, more than 800 did," the economist James Bessen pointed out in an influential article in 2015 about "how special interests undermine entrepreneurship."[11]

How can our leaders justify neglecting, and in some sectors pillorying, the greatest engine of job formation in history, the American entrepreneurial spirit? How many bankrupt businesses will it take to wake them up? How many startups deciding to set up shop in different countries? How many young people throwing in the towel on great job-producing ideas?

The specific policies that will maximize our entrepreneurs' ability to succeed are for another book—or another thousand. But surely, even in the highly polarized political climate we are now living in, everyone can agree that it is in the national interest that there be as many new companies as possible seeking breakthrough innovations and developing new and exciting services—and creating good-paying jobs—in every industry under the sun.

That turnaround is only possible if we fully appreciate the singular talents, skills, and mindsets of successful business founders—*the entrepreneurial difference*—so that policymakers and thought leaders will better understand the challenges they uniquely face and the circumstances that can better enable them to create the kinds of enterprises that will grow our economy into the twenty-second century.

In the end, it's those dreamers among us that will keep the American dream alive—for all of us.

Notes

1. Adam Heitzman. "How Entrepreneurship Might Be Genetic," *Inc.* (January 27, 2015). Accessed at: http://www.inc.com/adam-heitzman/how-entrepreneurship-might-be-genetic.html.
2. Milton Friedman, "A Friedman Doctrine—The Social Responsibility of Business Is to Increase Its Profits," *New York Times Magazine* (September 13, 1970).
3. Alvin Hansen, Address to the American Economic Association (1938).
4. Ian Hathaway and Robert E. Litan, "Declining Business Dynamism in the United States," Brookings Institution (May 2014). Also, "Young Entrepreneurs: An Endangered Species?" *Wall Street Journal* (January 2, 2015).
5. Jim Clifton, "American Entrepreneurship: Dead or Alive?" *Business Journal* (January 13, 2015).
6. John Haltiwanger, Ian Hathaway, and Javier Miranda, "Declining Business Dynamism in the US High-Tech Sector," E. W. Kaufmann Foundation, February 2014; Ben Casselman, "The Slow Death of American Entrepreneurship," *FiveThirtyEight* (May 15, 2014).
7. Olivia Zaleski, "Start-up Funding Deals Lowest in Four Years," *Bloomberg.com* (April 7, 2016).
8. Donna Kelly, "Endangered Species—Young Entrepreneurs," *Wall Street Journal* (January 2, 2015).
9. Thomas Friedman, *Thank You for Being Late: An Optimist's Guide to Thriving in the Age of Accelerations* (New York: Farrar, Straus and Giroux, 2016).
10. James Surowiecki, "Why Startups Are Struggling," *MIT Technology Review* (June 15, 2016).
11. James Bessen, "The Anti-Innovators: How Special Interests Undermine Entrepreneurship," *Foreign Affairs* (January/February 2015).

About the Author

Michael W. Sonnenfeldt is a serial entrepreneur, philanthropist, and political thought leader. He earned undergraduate and graduate degrees from the MIT Sloan School, where he was Phi Beta Kappa. By 25, Michael led the transformation of the Harborside Financial Center in Jersey City, New Jersey, the largest commercial renovation in the country at the time. He also was the founder of Emmes & Company, a real estate investment boutique that grew to over a billion dollars in assets. More recently, following his 30-year passion for the transformative potential of solar power, Michael became chairman of Carmanah Technologies, a public Canadian solar company focused on solar signaling and lighting for infrastructure projects, including offshore wind farms, marine aids to navigation, airfield ground lighting, and lighting for roadways, pathways, and parking lots.

Michael is founder and chairman of Tiger 21, the premier network of first-generation entrepreneurial wealth creators, whose members manage in excess of $50 billion in personal assets. Tiger 21 operates in 35 major North American cities and opened in London in 2017. Michael's own success as a serial entrepreneur, social venture capitalist, and founder of nonprofits that span international security, peacekeeping, climate defense, and the political arena places him squarely among his 500-plus peers at Tiger 21.

Michael is excited that 100 percent of the net proceeds of this book will be donated to the Tiger 21 Foundation, which is being formed to support young entrepreneurs who will be necessary to build the businesses and organizations that will support a vibrant middle class and a strong economy in the years to come.

Index